The Yoga of Nutrition

To my favorite doctor
Ruth Ellen Pearlman

Thanks to your kindness!
You make my life easier to live-
I hope that the author of this book
(OMA) my spiritual guide will be as
inspiring for you as he is to me.

Your patient
Evelyn McGehee

Happy Mothers Day
May 9-2010

Translated from the French
Original title: «LE YOGA DE LA NUTRITION»

Original edition:
© 1982, Éditions Prosveta S.A., ISBN 2-85566-179-X

© 1982, Éditions Prosveta S.A., ISBN 2-85566-189-7

Prosveta S.A – B.P.12 – 83601 Fréjus CEDEX (France)
ISSN 0763-2738
ISBN 2-85566-375-X

Omraam Mikhaël Aïvanhov

The Yoga
of Nutrition

Izvor Collection – No. 204

PROSVETA

Readers are asked to note that Omraam Mikhaël Aïvanhov's teaching was exclusively oral. This volume includes passages from several different lectures all dealing with the same theme.

TABLES OF CONTENTS

1. Eating: An Act which Concerns
   the Whole Man 7
2. Hrani-Yoga 19
3. Food: A Love-Letter from God 33
4. Choosing your Food 39
5. Vegetarianism 49
6. The Ethics of Eating 59
7. Fasting: A Means of Purification 75
   Fasting: Another Form of Nutrition 82
8. Communion 87
9. The Meaning of the Blessing 95
10. The Spirit Transforms Matter 103
11. The Laws of Symbiosis 115

Chapter One

EATING:
AN ACT WHICH CONCERNS
THE WHOLE MAN

Today we are going to talk about nutrition, eating, and what I have to tell you is something of the utmost importance which very few people know, even the most learned and most highly evolved. It is more than likely that to begin with you will not find it particularly interesting, but as you listen to me, above all as you begin to put these truths into practice, you will be obliged to recognize that they are capable of transforming your whole existence, of making it far richer and more beautiful.

Suppose that for some reason you have had to go without food for several days. At the end of that time you have become so weak that you cannot walk; you are incapable of the slightest movement. If at this point someone gives you a piece of bread or some fruit, however rich and learned you may be, it will be worth far more to you than all your learning and all your wealth combined. With the very first mouthful you will begin to feel your

vitality coming back. It is really wonderful how
fast this happens. That one mouthful sets in motion
so many forces and mechanisms that it would take
more than a lifetime to enumerate them all.

Have you ever stopped to think about the
power of the elements contained in food, or about
the fact that, when it comes to getting you back on
your feet again, a meal is always far more effective
than any thought, emotion or effort of the will?
You consider food to be important because your
instincts tell you that this is so, but on the level of
your intellectual or conscious life you do not attach
much importance to it, and yet it is the only thing
capable of restoring health and energy. Thanks to
the food you eat you can continue to act, to speak,
to feel and to think.

Initiates have always devoted a considerable
proportion of their time to researching the
question of nutrition. They have found that food,
which is prepared with unutterable wisdom in the
laboratories of the Lord, contains magic elements
capable not only of preserving or restoring both
our physical and our psychic health, but also of
revealing great wonders to us. But if we wish to
benefit from these magic elements we must first
know what conditions have to be fulfilled.

One cannot fail to recognize that the question of
food is in the forefront of people's preoccupations.
It is the very first problem that has to be taken care

of; this is what men and women work for every day of their lives. Indeed, it is what they fight for, many wars and revolutions have had no other cause than that of food. But this attitude toward food is simply an instinct that human beings have in common with animals. They have not yet understood the spiritual importance of the act of eating. In fact they have no notion of how they should eat. Watch people during a meal and you will see that they absorb their food mechanically, unconsciously. They swallow everything without chewing it. Their heads and their hearts are seething with chaotic ideas and emotions, and often enough they even quarrel among themselves while eating. No wonder they make themselves ill. All their functions are upset; nothing works as it should any more, neither digestion nor secretions nor the elimination of toxic wastes.

Thousands of people make themselves ill in this way without an inkling that their problems are caused by the way they eat. You need only observe what takes place in many families: before a meal no one has anything to say to the others; they are all busy reading or listening to the radio or doing their own little job. But as soon as it is time to eat, they all have some story to tell or some old score to settle, and the meal is spent in talking, arguing and quarrelling. After a meal of that kind they feel sluggish and sleepy and need a rest, or

even a nap, and those who have to go back to work
do so reluctantly and without enthusiasm. Those,
on the other hand, who know how to eat correctly
are clear-headed and alert after a meal.

Perhaps you are now wondering how you
should eat. Well, let me talk to you about how
initiates consider this question of eating. As they
wish to give themselves the best possible conditions
in which to receive the elements that have been put
into their food in nature's laboratories, they begin
by meditating and tuning in to their Creator. Above
all, they do not engage in conversation. They eat
in silence.

You must not think that silence during meals is
simply a monastic habit: sages and initiates also eat in
silence. They chew their first mouthful consciously
and for as long as possible until it disappears in the
mouth without being swallowed. One's frame of
mind when taking one's first mouthful is extremely
important, because it is this first step which triggers
the inner mechanism. You have to prepare yourself
beforehand, therefore, and make sure of having
the best possible conditions. Never forget that the
most important moment in every procedure is the
beginning, for it is the beginning which sets the tone
and releases forces which continue to be operative
throughout the activity. If you are in a harmonious
frame of mind at the beginning, the remainder of
your action will also be harmonious.

It is important to eat slowly and to chew your food well, because, as you know, this is good for the digestion. But there is another reason as well: the first organ to receive the food, is also the most important laboratory in the cycle of nutrition because it is the most spiritual. On a subtler level the mouth acts as a veritable stomach, absorbing the etheric particles and the finer, more powerful energies from food, while the coarser materials are sent on to the stomach.

The mouth contains some highly perfected devices in the form of glands on and under the tongue whose task is to extract the etheric particles from food. I am sure you have all had this experience many, many times: there you were, so hungry you were almost unconscious, and then you began to eat. With the first few bites, long before your food had been digested, you started to feel better and more energetic. How can it have happened so fast? It is thanks to the work that goes on in your mouth that your organism has already absorbed the energies and etheric elements needed to nourish the nervous system. Even before the stomach has received the food, the nervous system has been fed.

It should not surprise you to learn that etheric particles can be extracted from food. A fruit, for example, consists of solid, liquid, gaseous and etheric matter. Everyone is familiar with solid and

liquid matter. Fewer bother about the perfume,
which is already subtler and belongs to the realm
of air. But the etheric dimension of a fruit, which
is related to its colour, and especially to its life, is
something that is totally unknown and neglected.
Yet it is of the utmost importance, for it is by means
of the etheric particles in their food that human
beings nourish their subtle bodies.

Since human beings possess not only a physical
body but also other, subtler bodies (etheric, astral,
mental, causal, buddhic and atmic) in which reside
their psychic and spiritual functions, the question
arises of how to nourish these subtle bodies. Due to
ignorance, they are often left without food. People
know more or less what they should give their
physical body (I say more or less because most
people eat meat, which is very injurious to physical
and psychic health), but they have no idea what
they should give their other bodies: the etheric
or vital body, the astral body which is the seat of
feelings and emotions, the mental body, which is
the seat of the intellect, and even more remote, the
bodies of the higher self.

As I mentioned, you have to chew your food
well, but chewing benefits principally the physical
body. For the benefit of the etheric body you must
also breathe correctly. Just as air revives a flame
(you all know that if you blow on glowing embers
you can get a flame), a few deep breaths during

your meal will improve combustion. Digestion after all, like breathing and thinking, is a question of combustion. The only difference is in the degree of heat and the purity of the matter being burned in each case. While you are eating, therefore, you should pause from time to time to take a deep breath, and the better combustion which results will enable the etheric body to extract the subtler particles from your food. As the etheric body is the vehicle of vitality, memory and sensory perception, you can only benefit from its development.

The astral body, on the other hand, feeds on emotions, elements of still subtler matter than etheric particles. If you pause for a few moments to consider your food with love, your astral body will be ready to extract from it something even more precious than etheric particles. When the astral body is nourished by these elements it is capable of kindling very elevated feelings in you, feelings of love for the whole world and a deep sense of happiness, peace and harmony with nature.

Unfortunately, human beings are losing this sense of oneness with nature more and more: they no longer feel the protection, the solicitude, love and friendship of the objects around them, of trees, mountains or the stars. They are anxious and troubled. Even when they are safely at home and asleep at night, they have a vague sense of being threatened. This is a purely subjective impression, for in fact, they are in no particular danger, but something within them is disintegrating. They no longer feel the protection of mother nature because their astral bodies do not receive the nourishment they need.

Give your astral body the food it needs and you will experience an indescribable sensation of well-being which will inspire you to manifest yourself in generosity and good will, and when something important has to be settled, you will find that you can deal with it in a conciliatory spirit, with understanding and generosity.

In order to nourish their mental body, initiates fix their mind on their food; often, they will close their eyes so as to concentrate more deeply. And since they envisage food as a manifestation of the Godhead, they endeavour to study every aspect of it: where it comes from, what it contains, the qualities and virtues that correspond to particular types of food, and the entities that have had a part in preparing it (for invisible entities are constantly at work in every plant and every tree). With their mind absorbed in these thoughts, their food provides them with elements superior even to those of the astral plane. Clarity of thought and a profound understanding of life and of the world are born of meals taken in these conditions. When an initiate leaves the table after such a meal, his powers of comprehension are so enhanced, so luminous, that he is capable of undertaking the most demanding mental tasks.

Most people imagine that it is sufficient to read, study and think in order to develop one's mental capacities. But that is not so: study and reflection are indispensable, but they are not enough. If the mental body is to become strong and capable of prolonged effort, it too must be nourished by our meals.

We have to be quite clear about this: as the astral and mental bodies are respectively the vehicles of emotion and thought, we must give them the kind of nourishment they need if we are to be capable of assuming our responsibilities in the emotional and intellectual domains.

Over and above their etheric, astral and mental bodies, human beings possess other even more spiritual bodies: the causal, buddhic, and atmic bodies, the seats of reason, the soul, and the spirit, respectively. These three bodies also need nourishment, and you give them the food they need when you let feelings of gratitude toward the Creator flood your heart. A grateful heart – which is also becoming more and more rare among human beings – will open the gates of heaven, releasing a shower of blessings upon you. When this happens, the whole of creation will be unveiled before your eyes: you will see, you will feel, you will live. Gra-

titude is capable of changing crude matter into light
and joy, and you must learn to use it.

Once you have learned to nourish your three
higher bodies, the subtle particles that you extract
from food will be distributed throughout your
being: to the brain, the solar plexus and all your
organs. Then you will begin to realize that you
have other needs and other joys of a higher nature,
and you will see all kinds of possibilities opening
up before you.

When you have finished eating, do not leave
the table and go back to your discussions or your
work immediately. On the other hand, it is not
good to spend an hour or two in an armchair or
on a couch, either. If you go and lie down and
'have a rest,' as they say, in point of fact you
will not be rested, you will become sluggish and
your organism will become lazy. When you have
finished eating, stay quiet for a few moments and
take a few deep breaths so as to obtain a better
distribution of energy throughout your body. If you
do this, you will feel refreshed and ready for any
kind of work.

It is not enough to begin your meals well; you
must also conclude them as well as possible so as
to get the next activity off to a good start. Never
forget that each activity has its beginning and that
it is this beginning that is the key moment.

Chapter Two

HRANI YOGA

Today, many people who find their inner balance disturbed by the hectic pace of their lives turn to yoga, Zen, Transcendental Meditation or various relaxation techniques in the hope of regaining their balance and getting back on an even keel. Now, I am not saying that these methods are not good, but I have found a far simpler and more effective exercise, and that is to learn to eat correctly.

If you pay no attention to the way you eat, if you eat hurriedly in the midst of noise, discussions and nervous tension, what is the use of meditating or doing yoga exercises afterwards? Can you not see what a contradiction it is? Why can we not get it into our heads that every day, two or three times a day, we all have the opportunity to practise relaxation and concentration and to harmonize our cells?

If I ask you to make the effort to eat in silence (not only not to talk but to avoid the slightest noise with your utensils) to chew every mouthful a long time and to take a few deep breaths from time to time, above all, if I ask you to concentrate on the food you are eating and be grateful to the Lord for all these riches, it is because these seemingly insignificant exercises are actually some of the very best ways of acquiring true self-control. If you can master these lesser things you will be able to master greater things. When I see that someone is careless and clumsy in details, I can tell at once that he has lived in a state of disorder in the past, and that his present shortcomings are going to have a very negative influence on his future, for everything is connected.

Of course, it is difficult to refrain from talking in order to concentrate exclusively on one's food. Often, even if one manages to keep silence externally and to control one's physical gestures, there is still a lot of noise going on inside. Or, if one is peaceful and quiet within, then one's thoughts float away in all directions. And this is why I say that eating is a form of yoga, for to eat correctly requires attention, concentration and control.

In order to concentrate during meals, one must already have acquired the habit of concentrating in one's daily life. If you are constantly attentive and refuse to let negative thoughts and feelings invade your inner fortress, then the groundwork is already done and the rest will come easily. And now I can hear you saying, 'But do you mean that one has to work all one's life just to be capable of eating correctly?' Yes and no.

Obviously, you will not solve all your problems simply because you know how to eat correctly . If I am taking meals as a starting point, it does not mean that there is nothing more important, or that all the other things we do in a day can be done without attention or care. You must not misunderstand me. We have to be attentive and vigilant all day long, and we have to maintain that attention and that vigilance during meals.

A meal is a magical rite by means of which food is transformed into health, strength, love and light. Observe your own reactions: if you have eaten while you were agitated, angry or in a state of revolt, you will notice that for the rest of the day you will be bad tempered, irritable and biased, and if you happen to have any difficult problems to solve you will tend to take the negative view. Then you will try to excuse your attitude with, 'I can't help it. I'm too highly strung,' and in an attempt to calm your nerves you start taking pills – which will do you very little good. If you want to improve your nervous system, learn how to eat.

As soon as you find yourself with a plate of food in front of you, you must put aside every other consideration, even those that are very important, for the most important of all at that point is to eat according to the divine rules. If you eat correctly you will settle all your other problems in no time at all. Eating correctly, therefore, enables you to save both time and energy. Do not think that you can solve your problems more easily or more rapidly if you are over-wrought and tense; on the contrary, you will drop and break things, express yourself badly and make yourself thoroughly objectionable to others, and then you will have to spend days trying to undo all the damage you have done.

Most human beings have never realized that even the smallest actions in our everyday lives have great significance, so how can one get them to understand that meals can be an occasion for them to develop their intelligence, love and will-power? Everybody thinks that intelligence is developed through study, or perhaps by the trials and tribulations of life (when you are in a really tight spot some latent ingenuity awakens in you and helps you to find a way out of your difficulties). The qualities of the heart are developed by having a wife and children to protect and provide for. And the will can be developed by hard physical work, sports and so on. But can any of this be affected by the way one eats? The very idea seems utterly ridiculous. Well, those who think so have not understood very much yet.

The best time to begin to take care of the essentials, that is, to begin developing your heart, intellect and will, is at meals. There is no guarantee that everybody will have the opportunity to frequent libraries or attend university, that everybody will have a wife and children, or even that everybody will find occasions for a lot of physical exercise. But we can be sure that everybody will have to eat.

So, do you want to develop your intellect? If so, the opportunity is ready and waiting every time you need to handle the objects that are on the table. Try to pick them up and put them down gently, without touching anything else: this is an excellent exercise for the development of attention and foresight. When I see how people knock their knives and forks together or drop them on the floor I can see exactly what their intellectual shortcomings are. It makes no difference that they hold degrees from several universities, their intellectual deficiencies are still glaringly obvious to me. I mean it: what is the use of having a degree if you are incapable of judging distances?

Suppose, for instance, that you want to move your glass but you have not seen how it is placed in relation to other objects on the table: you move it and, 'Ding!' you knock it against something else. This is a mere detail, true, but it shows up a weakness which will manifest itself in far more important things in life. When someone is clumsy in his gestures at table it is a sign that he will blunder seriously in other areas of life as well. It

shows that he is lacking in a certain inner quality
of attention, and one can see, on a very small
scale, how he will behave in the important events
of his life. People like this speak and act without
thinking, they inconvenience and offend others,
and then they have to suffer the consequences for
years before they can put things right.

Look: I pick up this bottle which has just been
taken out of the refrigerator, and before starting to
fill my glass, I must remember that it is damp and
that if I do not dry it, it could slip and break the glass
or the plate. So, if I want to get a good grip on it I
have to wipe it dry. And it is the same in everything
we do, whether at table or in life. If an object is not
within your mental vision, within the reach of your
consciousness, you will not be able to control it: it
will not obey you. If you want to control an object
you have to begin by mastering it mentally: if it
escapes you, you will never be its master.

Also, before you settle down to your meal, try
to make sure that nothing is missing, otherwise you
may have to get up several times in the course of
the meal to fetch a knife, a plate, the salt, and so
on. This is something I have often observed when I
have been invited to a meal: my hostess is obliged
to get up twenty times because she has forgotten
this, that or the other. And yet we all know what is
needed, for it is something we do every day. But
no. People do not notice, and their entire life is

like that: they always forget something and have to interrupt their meal in order to go and get it. And if there is always something missing at table, it is a sign that in other areas of life they are equally inattentive and careless. In these conditions, how can they possibly hope to be successful?

In order to develop the qualities of the heart you must avoid making a noise or doing anything to disturb others, for they, too, need to calm down, to concentrate and meditate. A lot of people think, 'Oh, the others! I couldn't care less.' Well, it is precisely because of this attitude that the world is in such a sorry state: nobody thinks of others. People are incapable of living together because they do not respect or care about others. Eating together provides an excellent opportunity to develop and enlarge one's consciousness.

The sign that a human being is really evolved is that he is aware of belonging to a whole that is far greater than his own person, and that he takes care not to disturb the harmony of the whole by his own activity, thoughts, feelings and inner noise. Perhaps you will ask, 'What do you mean by inner noise?' All noise is the result of discord, and the noise within us, which is the result of our inner torments and revolt, disturbs the psychic atmosphere. Those who make a lot of inner noise do not realize that it is very harmful even to themselves, and that sooner or later it will manifest in their organism in the form of a physical or psychic illness.

When you are eating, remember to love your food: only then will it open up and give you all its treasures. You must have noticed how flowers react to the sun: when the sun is there to warm them they open their petals, and when it disappears they close up again. And food reacts in the same way. If you do not love it, it will give you practically nothing: it will lock up its treasures. But if you love it, if you eat with love, then it will open, pour forth its perfumes and give you all its etheric particles. You are used to eating mechanically, without love, simply in order to fill a void. But try to eat with love and you will see what a wonderful state of mind it produces in you.

I know very well that it is useless to talk of love to most people: they do not know what love is. They have no idea what it means to greet others with love, to walk and talk with love, to speak and look at others with love, to breathe and work with love, no idea at all. Love? They think it consists in sleeping with someone. No, as often as not, there is no love there at all. That is obvious. If people really knew how to love, heaven itself would be present within them.

So, as I have said, you can develop both your heart and your intellect during meals, but you

can also develop your will by acquiring the habit
of making controlled, rhythmical, harmonious
gestures. Gestures and movements are the domain
of the will. On days when you are feeling jumpy,
let your meals be an occasion to learn to calm
yourself. Chew your food slowly, pay careful
attention to your gestures, and you will find that
after only a few minutes you will feel quite calm
again. There are some very simple remedies for
nervous tension. If you start the day in a state of
agitation and begin working or talking without
doing anything to change it, the whole day will
be restless and agitated, and your energy will all
evaporate because you have forgotten to 'turn off
the tap.' So, pause for a moment in what you are
doing, do not say anything, do not move, and then
start all over again in a different rhythm and with
a different orientation.

The best time to begin to learn self-control
and self-mastery is during meals. Practise paying
attention to every little gesture you make so as to
be able to eat in absolute silence. I realize that I
am asking something that is almost impossible, but
you can do it. And all those who come here for
the first time will be amazed. They will say, 'But
it's impossible. I can't believe my eyes.' 'Well,' I
reply, 'in that case, believe your ears.'

When you eat in silence and peace, that state
of mind stays with you all day long. Even if you

are very busy and have to rush here and there, you need only to pause for a fraction of a second, and you can feel that peace still within you, all because you have eaten correctly. Otherwise, no matter how hard you try, even if you have a rest or try to speak calmly, you will still be nervous, tense and jittery.

Henceforth, nutrition, eating, will be recognized as one of the best forms of yoga, even though it has never been mentioned before. All the other yogas: Raja yoga, Karma yoga, Hatha yoga, Jnana yoga, Kriya yoga, Agni yoga, they are all magnificent methods, but it takes years of practice to obtain even very meagre results. Whereas with Hrani yoga (that is what I call the yoga of nutrition), results are extremely rapid; it is the easiest and most readily accessible of all yogas, and although it may still be on an unconscious level, every creature under the sun practises it. All the secrets of alchemy and magic are contained in this, the least known and the least understood of yogas.

So this is why, even if you are completely snowed under with work, you must never allow it to be a pretext for failing to develop your spiritual life. Every day, three times a day at least, you have a golden opportunity to tune in to heaven, to the Lord, for you have to eat three times a day. Everyone has to eat. Nobody has time to pray, read or meditate. All right. But you all have to take a few minutes every day for your meals. Then why not make the most of those few minutes and use them to work at your own perfection, to tune in to the Lord and send him a thought of gratitude and love?

From now on, let your meals be the occasion to effect this indispensable spiritual work. Many people think they are perfect because they live according to the laws of society: they do not cheat, they avoid harming others and they are very conscientious about fulfilling their professional and family obligations. And yet, in spite of that, the divine world is a closed book to them: they know nothing of the joy and happiness, the fulfilment and light that the divine life brings with it. They think they are perfect, but by what standards? It is a strange kind of perfection if it has no time for the soul and the spirit.

Naturally, we have to work in order to provide for our needs and not be a burden to others, but we also have to find a few minutes in which to nourish our soul and our spirit. We have been sent to earth with an important mission, but a lot of people forget this and are only interested in social success. And to think that they set themselves up as examples... Examples of what, I ask you? No light shines from them; they have never devoted one minute of their time to their spiritual lives or to improving themselves.

You are on this earth only for a very short time, and when you leave you will not be allowed to take your cars or houses or any of your wealth with you. All that will stay here, and you will leave with only your inner riches; these are the only acquisitions that you can keep forever.

Chapter Three

FOOD:
A LOVE-LETTER FROM GOD

Take a fruit, any fruit, and without going into the question of its flavour, perfume, colour, and so on, just look at it and realize that it is full of sunlight. It is a letter from the Creator, and everything depends on how we read this letter. Obviously, if we cannot read, we shall not benefit from it, and that would be a pity.

When a girl or boy gets a letter from their sweetheart, how fervently they read and re-read it; with what loving care they put it away among their treasures. But a letter from the Creator? It gets thrown into the waste-paper basket; it is not even worth reading. Man will be the very last creature to learn to read this letter; even the animals are more attentive than man. Yes, oxen and cows, for instance, read it through once and then they read it again, more attentively. That makes you laugh, and you think that it is not a very scientific explanation. Well, all right, call it chewing the cud or ruminating if you prefer the scientific word, but I say that they are re-reading their letter from God.

Food is a love-letter sent to us by our Creator
and we must learn to read it. To my mind it is the
most eloquent, the most potent of love-letters,
for it says, 'I love you, and I am giving you life
and strength.' More often than not, human beings
swallow their food without reading the words of
the letter, in which the Lord also says, 'My child,
I want you to be perfect. I want you to be like this
fruit, to have a delicious flavour. For the moment
you are sour, bitter and tough; you are not fit to
be eaten. You still have a lot to learn. Look at this
fruit: if it has reached maturity it is because it has
been exposed to the sun's rays. You must do the
same: expose yourself to the rays of the spiritual
sun, and the spiritual sun will work to transform all
your bitter, indigestible elements and will give you
bright, beautiful colours into the bargain.' This is
the message the Lord sends us through the medium
of food. You have not heard it yet, but to me it is
quite clear.

As we eat, our food speaks to us, for food is
condensed, concentrated light and sound. If your
thoughts are always straying you will not hear the
voice of light. Light is never separate from sound:
light sings, light is music. We have to learn to hear
the music of light, for it sings, it speaks, it is the
Word of God.

You could say, too, that nutrition is a form of
divination, for every being, every object emits

certain radiations, and the diviner is one who picks up and interprets these radiations. Food has picked up radiations from the whole cosmos. The sun, the stars and the four elements have left invisible but no less real imprints on it; they have impregnated it with all kinds of particles, forces and energies. Food even bears the traces left by the human beings who have worked in the fields and orchards or have simply walked through them. So food can talk to you about all its experiences; it can tell you tales of the sun and the stars, of angels and of the Creator. It can tell you about the entities which have cared for it day and night and filled it with special, beneficial properties for human beings, the children of God.

Even though nature sees that human beings are ignorant and half-asleep, she is so generous that she says to herself, 'Oh, never mind. Whether they are intelligent, conscious and awake or not, I will arrange things in such a way that their food gives them the strength they need to stay alive.' Like animals, unconscious human beings survive thanks to their food, that is obvious, but food taken in this way can give them only physical well-being. It cannot help them to grow spiritually

In order to extract the most subtle particles from our food, we have to be fully conscious and awake, and over-flowing with love. When this is the case, our organism is so perfectly prepared to receive the nutritious elements that the food feels

welcomed and willingly gives up all its treasures.
If you know how to welcome others lovingly, they
open up, they are ready to give their all; but if you
receive them ungraciously they close up. Put a
flower out in the light and warmth and it will open
and give up its scent, but if you leave it in a dark,
cold room it will close its petals. Food also opens
or closes depending on our attitude, and when it
opens it gives us the purest, most divine energies.

Chapter Four

CHOOSING YOUR FOOD

I

One day, one of my disciples who is a doctor had a telephone call from a woman whose husband was in bed with an acute bilious attack. 'Do you think it could be caused by something he ate?' she asked. 'We went to a wedding reception the day before yesterday.' 'Ah!' said the doctor, 'and what did you eat?' 'Well, I didn't eat much myself, because I wasn't hungry, but my husband has a good appetite and he ate well.' Whereupon she started to describe the menu. It was something unbelievable: sausages, salami, ham, pâté de foie gras, melon, sweetbreads with mussels, trout with almonds, rabbit with prunes, cheese, ice cream, cream cakes, fruit, various wines, champagne, coffee and liqueurs. 'Do you think any of that could have been bad for him?' asked his wife. A lot of people never make the connection between what they eat and the state of their health.

And yet the food we eat is the material from which we build our bodies, so you must not think

that you can consume whatever you like and
expect to be always in perfect health and as fit as a
fiddle. You have to understand that there is a direct
connection between what you eat and how you feel
afterwards. If you gorge on all kinds of different
materials, they will simply clutter your organism
which will be unable to get rid of them, and in one
way or another, you will end by being ill. You must
always be careful about what you allow to enter
your body.

Of course, some will quote Jesus who said
that it was not what entered into a man that was
important, but what came out of him. Well, you
have to know how to interpret Jesus' words. Would
it be reasonable to suppose that if you fill your
rubbish bin with refuse you will then be able to
get something clean out of it? Of course, if you
are an initiate you can eat anything, and thanks to
your high degree of evolution you will be capable
of transforming it and emitting it in the form of
light. Yes, but you have to be an initiate to do that.
Others, if they eat filth, will produce filth. Look at
the impurities coming from people's mouths and
eyes, simply because they have no idea that they
have the power to transform and sublimate their
food. They swallow dirt, and dirt is what comes
out of them. How can they possibly transform
anything when they have neither intelligence nor
purity, neither love nor kindness?

Jesus certainly never advised his disciples to eat anything and everything; it would be unthinkable for an initiate to give such advice. Only when you have accomplished great spiritual work capable of changing impurity into light are you free to eat whatever you like. And the reverse is also true: unless you have made up your mind to work at your spiritual development, even the best food will not have the power to transform you. What counts is the strength of your inner life, of your thoughts and feelings.

I know that dieticians recommend certain foods and advise against others. Of course, they are probably right, but it is not so much what you eat as the way you eat that is important. Eat whatever you want, but eat it correctly and in reasonable amounts and you will stay well. I have known quantities of people who followed a macrobiotic or some other special kind of diet, and as often as not it did not cure them; on the contrary, they continued to get weaker and weaker. I have no quarrel with macrobiotics, I admit that there is some truth in it, but when people think it is what you eat that is of first importance, I do not agree at all. No, food is only a means. What really counts is the psychic and spiritual life. The food you eat is of secondary importance.

Even the very best kind of food has never prevented evil, vicious people from trying to lay waste the world. Even vegetarianism is not all powerful: Hitler was a vegetarian. And then there are others who, in spite of the fact that they ate meat or other harmful foods, have become saints and prophets. They never went to school; they ate what they could find, and lived in ignorance of all the laws of hygiene. But they gave first place to the spirit, and with the handful of truths they knew, with an immense love for those truths and an inflexible determination to put them into practice in their lives, they achieved wonders.

But let us get back to the question of the food we eat every day. It goes without saying that we shall never find food that is absolutely pure here on the physical plane; we try to pick out the best, but one never knows exactly what one is buying. As far as thoughts and feelings are concerned, however, we can and must be very discriminating and pick out only the best thoughts and the best feelings and discard all the rest. Thoughts and feelings are the raw materials we use to form our subtle bodies, and if what we build is a slum – figuratively speaking – no prince or high-priest will come and visit us. The only visitors we'll have will be tramps. It is we who are the builders of our own etheric, astral and mental bodies and our destiny is determined by the quality of these bodies: we shall be visited by either luminous entities or entities of darkness; we shall be sent joys or sorrows; we shall know true glory or live in obscurity.

Man's future depends on how he eats. If you nourish yourself inadequately on the physical level you will look ill and your friends will ask what is wrong with you. This shows that the quality of your physical food can actually change your appearance. Well, the same is true of the quality of your thoughts and emotions. Certain thoughts and emotions are capable of rendering you more beautiful, while others, unfortunately, make you uglier. So why not pay attention to all this?

No transformation can take place in a human being unless better, more refined particles can be found to replace those of inferior quality. This is why it is not enough to eat in silence. We must fill the silence with the most elevated thoughts and feelings, for then it becomes so powerful and so full of magic that it can provide all the elements we need to nourish our subtle bodies. Silence is not emptiness: emptiness, a vacuum, cannot exist in nature. The universe is full of forces, materials and elements which become purer and more subtle as they reach the higher planes, and this powerful, magical silence is a mine from which we can extract great wealth.

The four elements (earth, water, air and fire), corresponding to the four states of matter, are contained in the food we eat every day. By eating, therefore, we are in contact with the angels that preside over the elements – the Angel of Earth, the Angel of Water, the Angel of Air and the Angel of Fire – and we can ask them to help us to build up our physical body and make it so pure and subtle that it may become a dwelling-place for Christ, for the living God.

Each of these angels represents certain specific qualities and virtues: the Angel of Earth represents stability; the Angel of Water, purity; the Angel of Air, intelligence, and the Angel of Fire divine life. If you are mentally in touch with these four angels while you eat, you will receive particles of a more highly spiritual nature with which to build all your subtle bodies, even your body of light. And when a man has fashioned that luminous body that the Scriptures call the body of glory, he becomes truly immortal.[1] The physical body cannot survive for long; after a while it has to surrender the elements of which it is made and return to the womb of mother earth. But in our body of light, our glorious body, we can live for ever.

The glorious body is given to all human beings as their birthright, but it is given to us in the form of an etheric seed, a minute germ, an electron, and our task is to give it form, to nurture and develop it. This is a process which exactly parallels that of gestation: just as a pregnant woman has to work for nine months on the germ received from the father, gradually adding the materials needed to form a living being who will perhaps be capable one day of making his mark on the whole world, similarly, on the spiritual level, we all have to apply ourselves to the task of nurturing and fostering the development of our glorious body. If we never think about it, never do anything to help it to grow and gain strength, it will remain hidden, buried and neglected. Fortunately it cannot die: it will wait until we become conscious and aware of it and begin to cultivate it, and then it will become powerful and luminous.

---

[1] See *«You are Gods»*, Collection Synopsis, Part. IX, chap. 4: «The Body of Glory»

The body of glory must be formed of particles
of the greatest purity, of the most intense vibrancy,
for only the intense vibrations of light are capable
of opposing the progress of disease and death, of
dislocation, corruption and disintegration. When
light triumphs in a human being, that human being
becomes immortal. This is why it is so important
that, through the food you eat, you learn to eat and
drink light in the unshakeable conviction that you
are thereby receiving new life.

Through nutrition you can communicate with
the angels of the four elements who will thus
become your friends and collaborators. When
eating, therefore, you must forget your worries,
your grudges and all negative thoughts, for it is
they that poison your food and make you ill. Link
yourselves to the angels of the four elements with
these words: 'Oh Angel of Earth, Angel of Water,
Angel of Air, Angel of Fire, give me your qualities
of stability, purity, intelligence and divine love.' In
this way you will enter into the new life.

Chapter Five

VEGETARIANISM

The subject of nutrition is extremely far-reaching, for it concerns far more than the food and drink that we imbibe at meals. Sounds, scents and colours are also sources of nourishment. The entities of the invisible world particularly are nourished by scents. The custom of burning incense in church, for example, comes from the very ancient knowledge that the spirits of light are attracted by pure scents such as incense, whereas the spirits of darkness are attracted by nauseating odours. But invisible spirits are sensitive not only to odours, they also find nourishment in sounds and colours – this is why many painters have portrayed angels playing musical instruments or clothed in pure, bright colours – and pure sounds and colours can be used to attract them.

Scripture says, *'Do you not know that you are God's temple?'* It follows, then, that we must take great care not to defile this temple by allowing impure elements to enter it. If human beings realized in what celestial workshops they had been fashioned they would pay far more attention to their food, for it contributes to the construction of these temples destined to be the dwelling places of God. But since they eat meat, most people are unfortunately more like graveyards full of corpses than temples.

All creatures, whether animal or human being, are attracted by one kind of food rather than another, and the choice they make is always very significant. If you want to see the results of a meat diet, go to the zoo and observe the carnivores and you will have your answer at once. In point of fact, though, it is not even necessary to go as far as the zoo; you only have to look around you to see innumerable human examples of all the animal species – even of those you will not find at the zoo, such as mammoths, dinosaurs and other prehistoric monsters. But let us be charitable and stick to the examples found at the zoo. There you will see the great flesh-eating animals, fearsome beasts that smell very strong, whereas the herbivorous animals are usually much less ferocious. Their food does not make them violent or aggressive, but the flesh eaten by carnivores is an irritant. Similarly, human beings who eat meat are more inclined to engage in brutal, destructive activity.

The difference between flesh foods and vegetarian foods lies in the relative amount of sunlight they contain. Fruit and vegetables are so steeped in sunlight that one could say they are a condensed form of light. When you eat a fruit or a vegetable, therefore, you are absorbing rays of sunlight, and light leaves very little waste. Whereas meat has only a low content of sunlight. This is why it decays so quickly, and anything that decays quickly is very injurious to health.

But the harmfulness of meat has yet another origin. When animals are being led to the slaughterhouse they sense where they are going and what is going to happen to them, and they are mortally afraid, terrified. Their terror disrupts the proper functioning of certain glands which then start to secrete toxic substances, and there is no way of eliminating these toxins from the flesh of the animal. Man ingests it in his meat, it enters into his own organism, and, naturally, it is not conducive either to good health or to long life. You will say, 'Oh, but meat can be so delicious!' Perhaps so, but you never think of anything but your own pleasure and satisfaction. The only thing that interests you is the pleasure of the moment, even if it has to be paid for by the death of countless animals and the ruin of your own health.

In addition, you must realise that everything we eat is like an antenna within us which picks

up certain specific wave-lengths. Meat tunes us in
to the astral world, in the lower regions of which
teem countless beings, all devouring and preying
on each other like wild beasts. By eating meat,
therefore, we are in daily contact with the fear,
cruelty and sensuality of animals. Those who eat
meat maintain this invisible link with the animal
world. They would be horrified if they could see
the colour of their auras.

Finally, anyone who takes the life of an animal
is assuming a very heavy responsibility; it is a
violation of the commandment, *'Thou shalt not
kill.'* Not only that: from Genesis we learn that
when God told man what he should eat, he said,
*'Behold, I have given you every plant that yields
seed... and every tree with seed in its fruit, you
shall have them for food.'*

When human beings kill animals for food they
are not only depriving them of life, they are also
depriving them of the possibilities for evolution
which nature had given them in this life. This is
why, on the invisible plane, each human being is
accompanied by the souls of all the animals whose
flesh he has eaten. They press in on him, claiming
satisfaction for the wrong he has done them: 'You
have deprived us of the possibility of evolving and
learning, so now it is up to you to take care of our
education.' Although the animal soul is not the same
as that of human beings, animals do have souls and

those who eat the flesh of an animal are obliged to put up with the presence of its soul within them. This presence manifests itself in states of mind that belong to the animal world, and this is why, even though a person may wish to cultivate his higher self, he finds it very difficult to do so. The animal cells refuse to obey his wishes; they have their own free will in opposition to his. This is why human beings often manifest in ways that do not properly belong to the human but to the animal reign.

As far as fish are concerned the question is quite different. For millions of years, fish have lived in conditions unfavourable to their evolution. This becomes obvious when one studies the structure of their organism: their nervous system is still extremely rudimentary. It is permissible, therefore, to eat fish, for this allows them to evolve. Also, they contain an element which is specially adapted to this era, and that is iodine.

The food we absorb passes into the blood-stream and from there it attracts entities with which it has an affinity. The Gospels say: *'Wherever the carcass is, there the vultures will gather,'* and this is true in the three worlds: physical, astral and mental. So, if you want to be healthy on the three levels, do not attract the vultures by eating carcasses. Heaven will never manifest itself through those who allow themselves to be invaded by impurities, whether physical, astral or mental.

Meat corresponds to a particular element in one's thoughts, feelings and actions. If, for instance, you dream that you are eating meat, you should be especially vigilant, for it means that you will be exposed to certain types of temptation: to commit acts of violence, to give way to sensual desires, or to harbour selfish, unjust thoughts, for meat represents all of these things: violence on the physical plane, sensuality on the astral plane and egoism on the mental plane.

Tradition tells us that before the Fall, Adam's countenance was radiant, and all the animals loved, respected and obeyed him. After the Fall Adam lost his radiance, and the animals became his enemies. If animals no longer trust human beings, if birds fly away when they approach, and if the whole of creation considers them hostile, there must be a reason. And the reason is that they have fallen from the spiritual heights where they once dwelt. In order to regain their first splendour they must once again submit to the laws of love and wisdom. When they do so, they will be reconciled with all the reigns of creation. The kingdom of God will have arrived.

On the surface it may seem that wars are caused by economic and political questions, but in fact they are caused by our wholesale slaughter of animals. The laws of justice are inexorable, and human beings are going to have to pay with their own blood; they are going to have to spill the same amount of blood that they have caused animals to spill. How many millions of gallons of blood that have been poured out on the earth are now crying to heaven for vengeance. And the vapours rising from all this blood attract not only microbes but also billions of maggots and pestilential entities from the invisible world. Most people do not know these truths, and many may refuse to accept them, but whether they accept them or not, I am bound to reveal them to you.

We kill animals, but nature is an organic whole, and by killing animals we are, as it were, affecting certain glands in that organism. When this happens, the balance of the organism is disrupted, and it is not surprising that before long war breaks out among men. Yes, human beings have slaughtered millions of animals for their meat, without realizing that on the invisible plane those animals are linked to other human beings, and it is they who will now have to share the fate of the animals. When we slaughter animals we are slaughtering human beings. Everybody agrees that it is time to establish the reign of peace in the world, that there must be no more wars. Yes, but war will go on just as long as we continue to slaughter animals, because by destroying them we are destroying ourselves.

Chapter Six

THE ETHICS OF EATING

Some people imagine that it is necessary to eat a lot to be strong and healthy. Not at all. In fact, the opposite is true. By eating too much we tire our organism and strain the digestive system beyond its normal capacity, thus causing an unnecessary overload which is almost impossible to eliminate. This is how a great many diseases come into being, simply because of this false notion that we need to eat a lot in order to keep well.

In point of fact, it is hunger that prolongs life. If you always eat until you are satisfied and leave the table feeling full, you will become sluggish and drowsy and lose whatever interest you may have had in perfection. Whereas if you leave the table with a little appetite left, if you refuse those last tempting mouthfuls, your etheric body will be stimulated to seek elements from higher regions to fill the remaining space. And within a few minutes, not only will you no longer feel hungry, but you will feel lighter, more vital and ready for work, because the elements the etheric body has found in space are superior in quality. If you always eat your fill and more, just for the pleasure of eating as so many people do, you will never really be satisfied. You will only succeed in upsetting your inner balance.

Those who eat too much create a state of saturation so that the etheric body is overworked and can no longer fulfil its function. When this happens, inferior entities of the astral world, seeing the abundance of food, rush in to partake of the feast, which you are offering them without realizing it. This explains why, in a very short time, you feel hungry and want to begin eating all over again to fill the void. Once again, your undesirable guests return, and in this way you become a magnificent lure that attracts the thieving, famished entities of the astral world who come and gorge themselves at your expense.

Of course, when I say that one should leave the table still feeling a little hungry, I am talking of only a very slight deprivation. If you deprive yourself systematically of an element that your physical body needs, the etheric body will be unable to supply the deficiency. But if, for instance, you reduce every kilo by about twenty grams, you will feel lighter and fitter thanks to the etheric element which adds itself to your material food.

Time and again I have had this experience of eating just a little less than my hunger clamoured for. Of course you will say, 'But it's so tempting to go on eating!' I know, it is very tempting. But what about your reason and your will power? Where do they come in? Is this not a golden opportunity to exercise them? Even on special occasions, at parties or receptions, you should be capable of saying no. Personally, I often have to say no. When I am invited to a meal, my hosts offer me all kinds of delicious dishes, in spite of the fact that I always warn them in advance that I only want a little salad, some vegetables and fruit. But, of course, no one pays any attention to that. They prepare a fantastic meal, and then when they see that I take very little, they are disappointed. Well, I cannot help that; they should have believed me in the first place.

I understood a very long time ago how much one loses when one lets oneself eat more than necessary: one pays for it by the loss of a subtle element that is far more precious than the flavour of the choicest dishes. And you too, you must learn to refuse when you are offered too much. If you do not refuse, you will be incapable of doing anything of value. If you stuff yourself, you will have to go and sleep it off in a corner while the spiritual work you should be doing is there, waiting for you. You have no right to be sleeping; the work must be done.

Of course it is up to each of you to know just how much food you need. People have different capacities, I know, and I have met some pretty extraordinary people in my time. Take Tseko, for instance: he was in the Brotherhood in Bulgaria, and his appetite left us all dumbfounded. He never seemed to have had enough to eat. He was a very nice, very obliging person, always friendly and smiling, and as he was very strong he always carried everybody else's baggage for them. When the brothers and sisters went up to camp on Mount Musala, Tseko would be loaded like a mule. The sisters, especially the older ones, all gave him their bags to carry, and he took it all in his stride without a murmur. If you turned around and looked back, you would see a mountain of gear climbing steadily along. Often during our excursions, he would carry the samovar used by the brothers and sisters to make tea, and he would carry it with the red hot coals and all. When the water boiled, steam hissed as it poured from the load on Tseko's back; he looked like some extraordinary kind of steam engine.

Of course, being so good-hearted he was everybody's favourite, and all the brothers and sisters liked to invite him to a meal. The only trouble was that he would eat everything on the table. If you wanted to have any food left over, you had to be sure that Tseko did not set eyes on

it, otherwise it would all disappear into the world's
most astounding stomach. When we camped at Rila
there were sometimes left-overs that had begun to
go sour and that had been put aside to be thrown
away, but when the sisters in charge of the cooking
went to get them, they had disappeared; Tseko had
eaten them. And no matter what he ate, he was
never ill. When the Master Peter Deunov saw what
an extraordinary creature he was, he would tell the
brothers and sisters who had lost their appetite to
go and see him; all they had to do was watch Tseko
eating and they found their appetite again. Yes,
Tseko was really phenomenal.

But that is not all: although he had never had any
education, he took it into his head to write poetry.
He thought that poetry consisted in finding words
that rhymed, so he wrote all kinds of meaningless
doggerel – but it rhymed. Naturally, when he read
us those 'poems' it was impossible not to laugh,
they were so comic, but that did not bother him. He
was never offended when we laughed at him. He
just went on imperturbably reading his poetry to us
around the campfire in the evenings at Rila. And
then, one fine day, he began to write real poetry,
and everybody was astounded. Nobody scoffed or
laughed at him any more.

After that he tried to compose music and
songs. Once again, everyone laughed at him: 'Can
you imagine? Tseko's become a composer.' But

before long we began to notice that the brothers
and sisters were humming his tunes and singing
his songs as they walked in the mountains near the
lakes of Rila.

Tseko was an electrician by trade, and one day
to our sorrow, we heard that he had received an
electric shock as he was working at the top of a pole
and had fallen and been killed. Every one mourned
him, and even now, fifty years later, I often think
of him. At any rate, I have never known a stomach
to match Tseko's.

But you are not Tseko. So you must accept
the fact that too much food is bad for your health.
Also, if you eat more than you need, you are
taking that which was meant for others, and if a
great many people do that, some will always have
too much and others will never have enough, and
this makes for an unjust imbalance in the world.
Conflict, revolutions and wars are all caused by
covetousness and greed, by the lack of moderation
on the part of those who accumulate wealth (food,
land, goods of every kind) that is denied to others.
But our collective conscience is not yet keen
enough to comprehend and foresee the long term
consequences and all the social disruptions that
this tendency can lead to.

This need to monopolize more than our share
leads to situations in which some people enslave

and subjugate others, or even wipe them out, at the first sign of resistance. Negligible though it may seem, it is the starting point of major catastrophes. It is important, therefore, to master, moderate and control this instinct as soon as possible. If you do not watch it, it will grow to such huge proportions in every area of your lives that it will become the source of the greatest possible tribulations.

So this is why disciples must learn not to overstep the mark where food is concerned. They must learn to stop eating before they are completely satisfied. When one is incapable of stopping, one feeds unnatural desires in oneself, and becomes like those who have a pathological need to accumulate more and more for themselves. They are already enormously rich, but their overweening ambition and lust are so immense that they are determined to possess the whole world.

Jesus said that it was easier for a camel to pass through the eye of a needle than for a rich man to enter the kingdom of heaven. For two thousand years, this saying has never been properly explained, and for anyone who does not know how Jesus reasoned, it does seem to be a strange thing to say. The point is that Jesus was not talking about the physical body; he was talking about the astral body. Owing to a rich man's excessive greed and avidity, his body of desire, or astral body, becomes bloated and swells up like an immense tumour, making it impossible for him to pass through the gates of the kingdom of heaven, wide though they may be. But a camel's astral body is very slim, because the camel is sober and content with very little. This is why it is capable of crossing the desert; when everybody else is overcome, the camel keeps going.

So you see, those who have never bothered about the question and who eat to excess are preparing tumours in their astral body which will make it impossible for them to pass through the gates of initiation. At the same time, they are running up a debt, because they are taking that which belongs to others. Their attitude is in contradiction to the laws of the spiritual world which demand a just and harmonious organization and sharing of resources.

If higher entities see that you have a coarse, egotistical mentality they will never accept you as one of them. They will say, 'Stay down there in the jungle where the wild beasts devour each other. That's where you belong.' And however bitterly you may complain that you are being bitten, stung and devoured, you will have to stay there and suffer. The gates of heaven will be closed to you until you learn to think in accordance with the philosophy of the Great Universal White Brotherhood.

You must understand that this question of food is not limited to physical food. The same laws prevail in regard to our thoughts and feelings. Lovers who 'eat' immoderately until they are satiated also end by having tumours in their astral bodies, and the gates of heaven will remain closed to them as well. The proof that the gates of heaven are closed to them is that they become completely glutted and disgusted; all inspiration abandons them, and they end by separating in bitterness and rancour.

So, get rid of the idea that it is healthy to eat a lot. Stupidly, some mothers think that if they love their children they have to stuff them with food. What nonsense! Instead of stuffing your children, you should teach them how to eat, teach them moderation, help them to understand that if they take more than they need, in one way or another they will be depriving others of what they need, if not on the physical level, at least on the astral or mental plane. One must think of others. How many of you, I wonder, think of sharing what you have when you are well off – particularly in the area of your thoughts and feelings? There are days when you are filled with joy and wonder, when you feel rich and happy. When you are blessed in this way, do you think of sharing some of that happiness with those who are suffering and desolate? No, you keep it all for yourselves.

You must learn to give away some of that wealth, some of that superabundant happiness, saying, 'Dearest brothers and sisters all over the world, what I have is so marvellous, I want to share it all with you. Take some of my happiness, take some of this light.' If you are sufficiently enlightened to do this, your name will be entered in the heavenly registers with the names of all those who are intelligent and full of love. In fact, whatever you distribute in this way will be added to your account in the banks of heaven, and later on, when you need it, you will be able to draw on it. Your joy will always remain within you, intact. No one will ever be able to take it away from you because you will have put it in a safe place.

Besides, have you never noticed that every time you want to keep some special joy for yourself and not share it with others, ill-intentioned entities of the invisible world are watching you and use one of your friends as a means to send you something to kill your joy. Even in the midst of great happiness something unforeseen occurs to rob you of your joy. Yes, simply because you did not think about sharing it. It never occurred to you to give it to the Lord or to the divine Mother, saying, 'This joy is yours, O Lord. Yours, O divine Mother. I am so stupid I do not know who to give it to, so I'll give it to you. Please distribute it for me.' And the Lord God and the divine Mother will distribute your joy for you and deposit part of it in the vaults of heaven. Accept this truth and benefit from it, for your own good and that of the whole world.

From now on, always try to stay within reasonable limits when you eat, because this is something which has repercussions far beyond the simple question of food. Besides, if you learned to eat with greater love and awareness, even if you reduced the quantity you ate by a half or a quarter, you would draw extraordinary energy from it. The energy that one single mouthful is capable of generating would be sufficient to drive a train all the way around the globe. Yes, just one mouthful.

Chapter Seven

FASTING

I

A Means of Purification

When you eat, your organism assimilates the useful elements and eliminates those that are foreign or harmful. But your organism may not always be healthy enough to recognize and sort out the two, either because you have given it too much food, or because there are too many impurities in what you eat. When this happens, wastes accumulate in the tissues of the various organs, and in particular in the intestines.

Even when it is pure, food leaves some waste in our bodies, and this is why it is good to fast from time to time so as to give our organism the chance to undertake the necessary cleansing process. Fasting is a method taught by nature itself: I am sure you all have observed how, when an animal feels ill, its instinct tells it to fast. It goes off and hides in a quiet spot, looks for some kind of grass or herb that will act as a purge, and waits until it is cured.

When you see dust lying thick on the furniture in your house, you know that you should do a little cleaning. But you seem to have difficulty in understanding that your own organism needs to be cleansed at least once a week, or that the millions of workers in your body (your cells), need a rest from time to time. Some illnesses show themselves in symptoms of fever, a runny nose, streaming eyes and skin eruptions; these are signs that a purifying process is going on. Since you could not make up your mind to do the work yourself, your organs are obliged to take it into their own hands.

Fasting is a very healthy habit, and if circumstances permit, it would do you good to fast for twenty-four hours once a week. During those twenty-four hours, try to devote yourself more particularly to spiritual work: tune in to entities of light, choose some inspiring music or reading, purify your thoughts and your emotions. Those who accept the discipline of fasting will find that, after a while, their body wastes do not smell nearly so unpleasant.

Do not be shocked by what I am saying; just imagine that I am your doctor. If you notice that your excretions and your perspiration have a strong and very unpleasant odour, it is a sign that you are ill, either on the physical or the psychic level. Perhaps you will say that the smell only depends on the kind of food you have eaten that day, but this is not so. In fact, observe the situation for yourself: if you are worried, angry or jealous for several days, you will find that the smell changes. Everything is reflected in the odours of the body.

It can also be very beneficial to fast for several days, but there again it is important to have suitable conditions. It is better, for instance, to fast during your holidays so as to be free to read, go for walks, meditate, pray and listen to music. Also, when we fast we nourish ourselves with air instead of food, so it is preferable to choose somewhere where the air is pure.

Many people suffer from various symptoms when they fast: backache, palpitations, headaches, and so on. This is a special language of nature, but as they do not understand it, they declare, 'Never again! Fasting is not for me.' Well, that is faulty reasoning. These feelings of sickness and physical discomfort are sent by nature to warn you that one day you will have to suffer in those same organs. If you want to know your weak spots, therefore, fast for a few days, and if you have pain in one of your organs, know that it is a warning: it is in that organ that you could be ill one day, so take precautions.

As long as it is done within reason, fasting is not dangerous and cannot do you any harm. Evidence of this can be seen in the fact that the discomfort is experienced especially during the first two days, and after that it disappears. If your discomfort were caused by the fasting, it would increase, whereas in fact you find that you are gradually filled with a deep sense of peace and tranquillity. No one has ever died from fasting for a few days from time to time, but millions have died from overeating.

To begin with, you may find fasting extremely uncomfortable because your organism does not know what to make of this sudden disruption of its routine. But do not draw the conclusion, on the basis of these first, temporary effects, that it is dangerous to fast. On the contrary, those who are the most liable to feel ill to begin with are those who most need to fast. They feel ill because of the unusual amount of toxic wastes which suddenly find their way into the bloodstream through the cleansing effects of the fast. Many people who judge only from outward appearances think that fasting will weaken them and make them look ill. Here, too, it may be the case to begin with, but after a few days one begins to feel better, one's problems clear up, and one becomes fresher, lighter and pleasanter to behold.

Those of you who want to fast will have to change your point of view. Instead of being alarmed if you feel unwell, you must just persevere until you feel better. If you break your fast at the first signs of discomfort, you will be making exactly the same mistake as those who start taking pills as soon as they feel a temperature coming on. Of course, they feel better immediately, but they do not realize that by getting rid of their fever in this way they are opening themselves to the risk of serious illness in the future.

Let your organism react freely in its own way. When it is clogged by waste it tries to get rid of that waste by producing a fever to dissolve it, and your temperature rises. You must put up with that temperature: it shows that your organism is cleansing itself. In fact, you can help the work along by drinking very hot, boiled water. Drink several mugs of hot water one after the other, and your temperature will soon drop. The hot water dilates the canals of the body, allowing the blood to flow more freely and carry the body's wastes to the organs of elimination and the pores of your skin.

It is also an excellent habit to drink hot water when you fast. Boil the water for several minutes and let the calcium settle before drinking it. Anybody who has ever washed greasy dishes knows that cold water is useless; you need hot water to dissolve the grease. Similarly, cold water leaves many material elements in our bodies intact, while hot water dissolves them and carries them away through the kidneys, the skin, and so on, leaving you feeling purified and rejuvenated. In fact it is a good idea to drink hot water every morning on an empty stomach. As hot water cleanses the

canals of the body, it is also an excellent remedy
for arteriosclerosis and rheumatism

At first, nobody enjoys drinking hot water, but
gradually one begins to feel how much good one
gets from it, and it becomes positively enjoyable.
Hot water is the most natural and the least harmful
remedy that exists, but nobody takes it seriously,
perhaps because it is so simple and so cheap. One
of our brothers cured himself with hot water once,
when his doctor had failed to cure him with other
remedies. When he went back to see his doctor, he
told him how he had cured himself, and his doctor
replied, 'Yes, I know that hot water can work
miracles in a great many cases, but I am sure you'll
agree that I cannot possibly charge my patients for
a consultation if the only remedy I prescribe is hot
water.'

During a fast the physical body naturally feels
deprived, but the etheric body compensates for
any shortages by contributing other purer, subtler
elements. The role of the etheric body is to care for
the physical body and keep it constantly supplied
with energy. Fasting, therefore, stirs the etheric
body to renewed activity, activity that takes place
on another level, allowing the physical body a
period of rest.

Of course, if you fast for too long, it will be the
etheric body which overworks while the physical

body does nothing, and that is not good either. The physical and etheric bodies are associates, partners, and if only one of them works it upsets the balance between them. Work must be shared fairly between the two.

In conclusion, I would like to say just a little about how to end a fast of several days. It is important to realize that one can kill oneself by suddenly resuming normal eating habits. The first day it is good to take a few cups of clear broth; the second day you can have some soup with dry toast, and on the third day you can begin to eat normal, light food, and not too much of it. If you do this you will be in no danger.

After a fast of this kind you will experience new, subtle sensations; you will have revelations; above all, you will feel younger and lighter, relieved of a burden, as though the matter that had been weighing you down had vanished, as though all wastes and impurities had been burnt away.

There are many very interesting aspects to be studied in this question of fasting. But ignorance and fear prevent people from following the example of so many spiritual and mystical figures in the past, and from renewing and regenerating themselves by fasting.

Another Form of Nutrition

The truth is that this question of fasting goes much further than you imagine. All our problems are caused by the impurities left over from previous lives. Each sin or failing in the past has left debris behind it, and our troubles are due to all this accumulated waste that has never been cleared out. When you fast, you rid yourself of much of this harmful accumulation; many of your darkest zones receive an influx of light, and you feel joyful and more buoyant. This is why all religions and spiritual teachings have recommended fasting.

Fasting is not a question of 'mortifying the flesh' or of depriving oneself; on the contrary. The main purpose and function of fasting is to nourish oneself. When you deprive the physical body of food, the other bodies (etheric, astral and mental) begin to work more actively. For there is a principle in the human being that defends itself, that refuses to let itself die, and if the physical body is short of food, it sounds an alarm. When the entities that dwell within and watch over the health and well-being of your organism hear the alarm, they come to your rescue and bring you sustenance from higher spheres to make up for what is lacking. Then you begin to absorb the elements you need from the atmosphere and to feel yourself nourished. And if at this time you hold your breath for a few seconds, still higher entities from the astral and mental regions will come and bring you food.

Esoteric tradition tells us that the first man lived on fire and light, but that as the process of involution advanced and he found himself obliged to descend into the lower regions of matter, he needed to eat gradually denser and heavier foods, until he was eating the same kind of fare that human beings eat now. And this is why initiates, who know that our present diet is the result of involution, endeavour to return to man's primeval conditions by teaching themselves to assimilate ever subtler elements. It is as though they rejected first the stomach, then the lungs. In this way their mental faculties are freed. But this takes long and arduous training, and even in India very few yogis achieve complete control of their breathing. Those who do so can float at will in the Akasha, in cosmic ether; they possess the fullness of knowledge and are totally free.

So man has descended from celestial regions through a process that is known as involution. Progressively, as he approached the lower regions of the material world, and as the distance that separated him from the primal fire became greater, he was clothed in gradually denser bodies until he acquired the physical body as we know it today. In winter, when we put on additional layers of clothes to protect us from the cold, it is a faithful reflection of the process of involution. And now, in order to climb back to where we came from, we have to learn to undress, symbolically speaking – that is, to strip ourselves of all that weighs us down. Fasting is one way of recapturing that primordial lightness and purity.

But fasting is not only a question of abstaining from physical food. It is also a question of renouncing certain cumbersome thoughts and feelings. Instead of always trying to take – to absorb, devour and accumulate things – we have to learn to give, to give up things and thus free ourselves. It is the accumulation of excess baggage that pulls us down. Every thought, feeling or desire that is not spiritual in nature clings like hoar-frost on the bare branches of the trees in winter. Only the spring sunshine can melt the ice and restore us to our true condition. As soon as we manage to slough off all those useless accumulations, we feel vivified by an inrush of divine breath.

Those who are bent on stuffing their hearts or their heads with everything they can lay hands on have no room for God or his angels when they come to visit them. But now, do not misunderstand me: I am not saying that you should no longer use your stomach, lungs or intestines. Not at all! To destroy one's body is no way to reach an understanding of truth. You have to preserve the whole of your body – head, heart, lungs, stomach, and all the rest – but you have to learn to create harmony among all your different parts. That is the true meaning of fasting.

Chapter Eight

COMMUNION

One of the essential practices of the Christian religion is the rite of Communion. Jesus was not the first to institute this practice; it existed centuries before his time, for the Book of Genesis relates how Melchizedek, high priest of the Almighty, went out to meet Abraham with gifts of bread and wine.

But communion must not be restricted to the occasional taking of a host consecrated by a priest. In reality, every human being must be a priest, one who sacrifices; this is the inner vocation common to us all, and each one of us is going to have to answer for it before the Lord. Every day of our lives we have to officiate in the presence of our cells and give them bread and wine. If you are conscious of your role, your cells will receive true communion from you (that sacred element that will help them to accomplish their daily tasks) and the contentment and satisfaction they feel because of work well done will be such that you too will share it.

To understand the mystery of the Last Supper we have to take nutrition as our starting point. It is true that breathing and, above all, spiritual exercises such as meditation, contemplation and identification are all forms of communion, yet we must begin by understanding nutrition. Not everybody has the necessary conditions or even the capacity to meditate or to contemplate, but we all eat every day. So we must all start by understanding communion on the physical level.

Communion is an exchange: you give something, and you receive something else in return. You may think that when you eat, you do no more than receive your food, that there is no giving on your part, but this is not so: you also give something to your food. If you do not do so, it is not true communion. True communion is a divine exchange. The host gives you the blessings it contains, and if you take it without giving the necessary love and respect in return, then it is not communion; it is a dishonest act. When one takes one must also give. You must give the host respect, love and faith, and in return it will give you the divine elements it possesses. Those who have never received the host with this attitude of sacred respect are not capable of being transformed. It is not the host itself that changes us; it is the trust and love we give it.

To be in communion with the Lord you must give him your love, gratitude and devotion. Not that the Lord needs what you give him – he is so rich he can well do without it – but it is you who will benefit, for by endeavouring to give him something of your heart and soul, you awaken certain spiritual centres in yourself and let in a flood of divine virtues.

But let us get back to the question of food. While preparing a meal, you must handle the food consciously and remember to impregnate it with your love. Speak to it. Tell it, 'You bear the life of God within you, and I love and esteem you. I know what wealth you possess. I have a large family, millions and billions of inhabitants who all need you, so please be kind and give them that life.' If you get into the habit of communicating with your food in this way it will become strength and light within you, because you will be communicating with nature herself. Also, you will begin to see that true communion has a much broader significance than that which the Church normally attributes to it.

Besides, is it intelligent to think that you have to receive a host in order to communicate effectively with the Lord? No host has ever succeeded in transforming a human being. You can swallow wagon-loads of hosts and still be the same lazy, thieving good-for-nothing. It all depends on your level of consciousness. When you are conscious that the life of God himself is concealed in your food, then, when you sit down to a meal you will be like the priest who blesses the bread and wine, and every day, at every meal, you will be in communion with divine life.

Nobody has greater understanding and respect for the sacred than I, and this is why I invite you to practise this every day, for I know that the day will come when each one will be a priest of the Lord. Those who understand God's creation, who love and respect all that God has made, are priests. Whether they have been ordained or not makes no difference; they are priests consecrated by God himself. God is greater than everything that exists; he is no one's servant; no one can lay hold of him and force him to confine himself to a host and then distribute him as they please. Besides, why use violence on the Lord, since he has always been present most willingly in the food we eat? He does not like such attempts to use force on him, and often, when we want him to be present, he is not.

The exaggerated importance given to the host has led people to neglect the question of food and forget that it too can be a bond with God. And now, here am I to open your eyes and tell you that food is just as sacred as the host, because all of nature, God himself, made it for us out of his own quintessence, and in view of that, what can the blessing of a priest add to it?

The Church has so deformed human beings that there is no longer any way of getting them to appreciate the wonders created by God. They are full of awe at their own creations, but they are not interested in what God has created; they are above such things. Of course, if you question priests they will never admit that they consider themselves superior to God, but in practice it is exactly as though they thought they were. Instead of saying, 'Respect all life, my children, for everything is sacred; everything in nature is a talisman placed there for us by God himself,' they tell the faithful to respect only their own rites and ceremonies: the host, the Rosary, medals and so on. The rest is unimportant.

I have no wish to depreciate either the role of priests or the importance of sacramental Communion. I only want to open up new horizons before you, so that you may see that communion is not merely important, it is indispensable. We need to communicate every single day. If you communicate only two or three times a year, what do you think you can possibly change in yourself? Nothing! Absolutely nothing! Your cells will be just the same and you yourself will never change. If we want to transform our physical body, which is so dense and stubborn, we have to keep working at it every single day by means of our thoughts, faith and love, and one day, at long last, this carcass will begin to vibrate.

We must not allow the rites instituted by the
Church to hide true religion from us. People often
look only through the spectacles of one religion, one
philosophy, one clan, and all the rest is neglected.
What is the use of belonging to a religion if that
religion hides the splendour of God's creations and
deprives human beings of any real possibility of
returning to him?

Chapter Nine

THE MEANING
OF THE BLESSING

Most of the food we these days eat is contaminated by various toxic chemicals; it is virtually impossible to buy anything that is really fresh and pure. Fruit and vegetables are grown in soil tainted by harmful fertilizers; fish is taken from the waters of polluted seas and rivers. It will soon be impossible to live on this earth. But most people simply do not care that others die because of the poisons they produce, as long as their business prospers and they make a lot of money.

And yet it largely depends on each one of us whether or not the food we eat is assimilated by our organism, and the prayers and blessings we say before meals are designed to have a beneficial influence on our food and prepare it to be properly assimilated. These formulas and prayers cannot add the tiniest scrap of life to food, for God has already infused life into it through the action of his servants, the sun and the wind, the stars, earth and water. If it were possible for a human blessing to

introduce divine life into an object, why should we
not bless and eat pieces of wood, stone or metal?
It is true that when we bless a stone or a piece
of wood or metal, we are instilling a certain kind
of life into it, but it is not a kind of life that can
nourish human beings. They may be able to use it
for some other purpose, but not as food.

'In that case,' you might say, 'it is surely
pointless to bless our food. It does no good.' No,
it is not pointless, for as I have already said, the
words and gestures of the blessing wrap the food
in emanations and fluids which prepare it to vibrate
in harmony with those who are going to eat it, and
an adaptation takes place in their subtle bodies
which enables them to receive and benefit from
the properties contained in the food.

This question of blessing food is not properly
understood. Even priests do not really know why
they have to bless the wine and the hosts. Those
who established these rites in the past were aware
of their magical significance, but now all that has
been lost. The real purpose of the blessing is to
make a friend of one's food, for you must realize
that food has its own form of life and that its
vibrations are not always in tune with ours. We
have to magnetize it, give it some of our particles
so as to change the rhythm of its own particles and
ensure its friendship. Only then will it open up and
pour out its riches for us.

When two people meet for the first time, their vibrations are so different that they sometimes have difficulty tuning in to each other sufficiently to understand each other. But as time passes, a relationship of exchange, a kind of osmosis takes place, and they begin to vibrate in unison. And this is what happens with our food: if you start eating without having prepared yourself inwardly, your food will remain foreign to you and will not do you as much good as if you tried to make friends with it in advance. You have often seen me holding a fruit in my hand for a moment before eating it; I am transforming its etheric body and asking it to open itself to me.

One can smile at food just as one smiles at an animal one is trying to tame. Animals, plants, all creatures need to feel love before they are willing to make friends. And this is true of food and even of medicine: if you want a medicine to be properly assimilated by your organism and really do you good, you have to influence its etheric matter. Even a stone vibrates when you hold it, and its vibrations will be either friendly or hostile to you. If you know how to make a friend of a stone, it will protect and even heal you. This law can be seen in every area of existence. Look at how it operates between boys and girls. To begin with they are strangers and ill at ease; the girl, sitting bolt upright in her chair, as innocent and honest as can be, is a sight to behold.

But the boy only has to give her a drink and put on a sentimental record and all her reserve falls away; she becomes his 'friend.'

When you put on a new pair of shoes for the first time, you do not feel at home in them; they are stiff and tight. But after a while they get used to your feet, as it were, and loosen up. And to begin with, when you move into a new room or a new house, you feel a little lost; the place is foreign to you. But there again, you soon begin to feel at home and are even glad to get back to your room because it is full of the vibrations you have put into it.

The strange thing is that where food is concerned, nobody seems to think that anything needs to be done. And yet, before it reaches your plate your food has lain about in all kinds of places. It has been handled and packed and shipped to market; it is a total stranger. But if you take a fruit, hold it with respect and look at it lovingly, it will become your friend and vibrate quite differently. It is like a flower which opens its petals and offers you the gift of its perfume. The secret to opening the treasure-house of food is warmth, the warmth of love. This is why, if you do not like any particular kind of food, you should not eat it, for it will be an enemy in your organism. Never eat anything you do not like.

And now, try this exercise: before you eat a piece of fruit, hold it in your hand, talk to it softly (if not out loud, at least in your thoughts), and something in that fruit will be transformed. It will be much more friendly toward you, and when you eat it, it will begin to work for you.

Learn to awaken all those powers within you that have been put to sleep, chloroformed, by centuries of inertia and stagnation. Concentrate, meditate, pray and exercise your faculties. Always keep alive that desire to add something more to your life, something purer and subtler.

Chapter Ten

THE SPIRIT
TRANSFORMS MATTER

I

Solar energy exists in concentrated form in the fruit and vegetables we eat. We have to learn, therefore, how to extract that energy and send it to all the centres of distribution in our bodies. This is something that can only be done by the power of thought. The only way we can release all that energy imprisoned in our food is by consciously concentrating on it in our minds. This is, in fact, a process identical to that which is applied in a nuclear power station. If we really knew how to eat we would need no more than a few mouthfuls; they would give us enough energy to move the whole universe.

Fission takes place not only in the stomach, but also in the lungs and the brain. Perhaps the mention of the brain will surprise you, but where do you suppose an initiate finds the energy for his incessant meditations and ecstasies, when he sends waves, currents and flames out into space? That energy comes from his brain. And yet, if you weighed his brain you would find that its mass does not change. A few particles of matter in the brain disintegrate, and this disintegration produces the psychic energy that reaches out to the entire world.

Contemporary science has discovered atomic fission, but the process has been known to initiates for thousands of years. Initiates have never revealed it to others, however, because they recognized the danger of doing so; they knew that human beings were not yet masters of their own instincts, and that they would use these discoveries to annihilate all around them – which is exactly what is happening today. But in the future, when human beings are more highly evolved, they will have access to the great mysteries of nature and will know how to draw energy from the ocean, from the air, from minerals and trees, then they will be capable of prodigious achievements.

For the time being, try at least to understand how much energy you can get from food if your mind participates in the nutritional process. Nutrition is a war between the human body and the food that is destined to be assimilated, and the parts that cannot be assimilated are discarded. Food has to be crushed and destroyed before it can be properly absorbed; our organism is obliged to destroy in order to construct. All this happens automatically, of course, without our even being aware of it, but by our thoughts we can also act consciously on our food, cause it to open up, and draw from it the energies that will enable us to accomplish our spiritual and material work more easily.

II

Why do human beings have to eat? Why do all creatures have to eat? If you ask people this they will probably tell you that you have to eat to keep up your strength. That is true, but surely there must be some other reason as well. We rarely do something for only one reason, with only one goal in mind; if we eat it is not simply in order to stay alive.

Let us take the example of the earthworm: it swallows and then eliminates soil. By putting the soil through their digestive tract, worms change it and add something to it, with the result that it is more fertile. And human beings do the same with the food they eat. Since human beings are creatures endowed with life, feelings and thought, they belong to a far higher level of evolution than the matter they ingest, and as this matter passes through them, it is transformed, vivified, refined and spiritualized.

All beings need nourishment – plants, animals and human beings – and in the process of nourishing themselves they cause matter to evolve by giving it elements that were previously lacking to it. It is as though each kingdom or order in nature had a duty to feed on the lower kingdoms in order to advance their evolution. And on a level higher than ours are beings which digest us as well in order to transform us. Yes, the outward form is different, but the process is exactly the same. The whole of life is an unbroken chain of exchanges between the organic and the inorganic worlds, between the spiritual and the material.

Exchanges exist in every area. Why do intelligent, educated people spend time instructing the ignorant? Why do those who are virtuous, generous and kind try to help criminals and delinquents? Why do the strong help the weak and the rich help the poor? Evolution is only possible if there is interaction and exchange between two opposite poles. And this is also the reason we have to eat. Cosmic intelligence could certainly have devised other ways, but this is the one it chose: it decided that, in order to advance and evolve, every creature had to be absorbed and digested by those of the level immediately above its own.

I mentioned the example of earthworms: the soil eliminated by a worm is already more highly elaborated than when it was first absorbed. It is alive, as it were, with an element communicated by the worm. And if worms have received the mission to process the whole earth by putting it through their digestive tract and thereby improve it, why not human beings, too? So you see, human beings and worms are co-workers. Although they do not know it, their task is identical. They have signed a contract on high before coming down to earth; human beings in one form and worms in another, and both have committed themselves to working with matter in order to transform it. Does the idea of signing a contract amuse you? Well, laugh if you like. It will do you good.

When man's own material elements, the particles of his physical body, reunite after death with the four elements (earth, water, air and fire), they are more intelligent, more alive and more expressive than when he first acquired them, and if he has lived honestly they will be used for other forms, other creations of a higher order. If on the other hand, a man's physical elements have been debased because of the brutish, criminal life he has led, they will serve only to form simple, crude creations. What a responsibility for human beings!

Yes, human beings are responsible for what they leave behind when they go; they are responsible for all the particles of their bodies that they have impregnated either with light, love, goodness and purity, or on the contrary, with criminal vibrations. If people commit crimes or leave debts behind them, they cannot be prosecuted once they are dead. How could the police find them to bring them to justice? But death does not put an end to their responsibility. On earth, death solves a lot of problems, but on the other side, death settles nothing, and human beings can still be prosecuted for the evil they have left behind them, for all their evil thoughts, feelings and actions. Most people are unaware of the truth of this; they have no idea how great their responsibility is. And yet an awareness of one's personal responsibility is the highest form of conscience.

Eating, drinking, breathing and working – these are all activities by means of which we transform matter and try to give it something of what we ourselves possess: life, love and intelligence. Plants feed on minerals; animals feed on plants; human beings feed on animals. And who feeds on human beings? That is a question that no one ever wonders about.

In fact there are two kinds of creatures that feed on human beings. Among human beings there are those who eat the flesh of animals, but there are also those who are content to eat only what animals produce: milk and eggs. Entities of the higher worlds do not eat the flesh of human beings; they eat only what humans produce: their emanations, their

thoughts and feelings. And depending on whether
the thoughts and feelings of human beings are good
or evil, they provide nourishment either for the
angels or for entities from the lower regions. The
angels in turn serve as nourishment for archangels,
the archangels for Principalities, and so on, all the
way up the hierarchical ladder to the Seraphim,
whose emanations nourish Almighty God.

From time immemorial, initiates who were
in possession of knowledge that they could not
hand on directly to the masses have always used
images which we have to learn to interpret. In the
Bible it says that burnt offerings were 'a sweet
savour' to God. Just imagine how God's nostrils
must have twitched with pleasure at the smell of
roasting meat and burning fat. But this was an
image intended to teach us that men's spiritual
emanations (represented by the victim offered in
sacrifice to God) could serve as nourishment for
the whole hierarchy of higher beings and even for
the Lord.

For God, too, eats. Since we are made in the
image of God and we eat, this must mean that God
also eats. Obviously, God's eating is not like ours,
with a mouth, teeth, a stomach and intestines and
so on. In God all is so sublime and pure that we
cannot have even the faintest notion of how he
eats; we can be sure only that he does eat. If it were
not so, why should the Bible have written such

idiotic things – that God delighted in the scent of the victims offered in sacrifice – if there were not a deeper truth underlying these words?

Our job is to put matter through our digestive system in order to give it life. This is why we eat. Have you ever tried to calculate how much one human being eats during a lifetime? If you multiply that by all the human beings who have ever existed in the millions of years of the history of humanity, you can see that this must have changed a number of things throughout the world. The world is simply not the same as it was. All the more so as there are so many very generous, conscientious people who accomplish their mission with such ardour that they eat five or six copious meals a day in order to contribute to the evolution of matter. Now these are the kind of people who should be encouraged and rewarded! Yes, really... Look at the magnificent job they do! How many pigs, turkeys, chickens and rabbits disappear every day thanks to them? Their only aim is to improve creation; we must not forget that. Whereas all those weedy little vegetarians, nibbling away at their salads, what have they ever done to earn our gratitude? They will never transform as much matter as all those ogres.

In fact, of course, it is not simply a question of putting matter through one's digestive system,

through one's stomach, but also through one's
lungs, heart and brain. The life we have received
does not stagnate within us: it flows, it is always on
the move, always new and different, always fresh.
So eating is not the only way in which we can
improve matter; we can do so by every one of our
actions: seeing, walking, working, by everything
we do. Yes, a true understanding of nutrition goes
a very long way. If we want to be useful to the
whole of creation, if we want to be among those
who contribute something divine to the entire
world, we must learn to live perfect lives so as to
impregnate everything around us with light. And
those who have this ideal of rendering everything
more alive, more luminous and more beautiful
transform themselves, for all their energies and
faculties are mobilized for this work, and they
receive help from any number of collaborators
from the invisible world.

Chapter Eleven

THE LAWS OF SYMBIOSIS

I

It is amazing to see how human beings, who are conceited enough to think that they can plumb the depths of the mysteries of Creation, totally neglect something as important as nutrition, into which God has poured all his love and wisdom. If one studies the laws that govern the process of nutrition one realizes that they are in effect throughout creation. They govern the relationship of exchange between the sun and the planets; they apply in all areas of life; in particular, they apply in the area of love. Yes, the laws that govern conception and gestation are identical to those that govern nutrition.

In everything we eat, whether it be fish, fruit, vegetables or cheese, there is always something that has to be discarded: bones, peel, a crust, a core, and so on. And even if there is really nothing that has to be thrown away, we at least have to wash or wipe it clean. In other words, before eating we have to take certain precautions so as not to wound our palate, break a tooth or damage our stomach. Knowing this, why do we not do the same in life itself? Before creating a bond with someone, before taking someone into our heart and soul, why do we not examine the question of whether he is fit to be swallowed and digested? You will probably say, 'But I love him.' Yes, I quite understand that you love him. But that kind of love is blind; it is not real love. Real love is enlightened; it is never contrary to wisdom.

People create bonds with others and kiss and embrace them without preparation of any kind, without washing or cleansing themselves, without clearing out the filth that has accumulated in their hearts and souls as they scrambled through the chimneys of life. Initiates behave quite differently: on first meeting others they envisage them as 'juicy fruit,' but as fruit that needs to be washed and peeled before it is fit to be 'eaten.'

The great difference between initiates and ordinary human beings – who possess neither light, nor wisdom, nor knowledge – lies in the way in which they associate or establish an exchange with others. Ordinary people behave like cats – which swallow mice whole, whiskers, intestines and all – and then weep and lament and declare that they are unbearably unhappy with their wife, or that their husband is a monster. But then why did they behave like cats in the first place. Why were they in such a hurry to 'eat' that man or woman? In other words, why did they associate with them and accept their thoughts and feelings, their breath and their aura, without reflection?

Now, analyse yourselves and review your life, and you will see that you have never looked any further than the outward appearance, the little external details of those to whom you felt drawn. You have never stopped to find out what their inner motivations were, how they felt about things, what kind of thoughts and ideals they cherished. Initiates, on the other hand, are very difficult to please, and rightly so. They have understood the lesson that nature gives us every day by means of our food. They know that we have to behave in accordance with the same laws in the psychic life. Every day we peel, wash, clean and discard on the physical level, and we still have not understood that nature is teaching us to do the same on the psychic level. Have you never seen how an adoring mother, a mother who would do anything in the world for her little boy, will send him to wash and clean up after playing in the mud before she will kiss and cuddle him? Why does she not kiss him straight away, mud and all, since she loves him? The great book of living nature is there before your eyes. For the wise its pages are open, for others it remains closed.

Three times a day you have a meal. Three times a day you pick out what is edible and discard the rest, and yet you tie yourself for life to the first person to come along, without getting to know him or her, thus running the risk of poisoning your whole life. The Lord is the only one that we can safely love before getting to know him. With human beings you must always get to know them before loving them, in other words, before eating them, before admitting them into your inner sanctuary. But if you do not love God from the very beginning, you will never get to know him. The same law applies in the case of a great Master: if you do not begin by loving him, you will never get to know him, and he will remain a closed book to you.

Obviously, the question now arises of how to love. Most people love a Master as they would love a lake in which they wash away all their grime. It never occurs to them that others may want to come and drink from the lake – and what will they be obliged to drink with their water? Most people who go to see a Master unload all the filth of a lifetime on to him. He then has to discard or transform these impurities, and all of this gives him extra work. If even a Master is obliged to cleanse himself, how much more so must others do the same. Oh, but in their opinion they do not need cleansing. They have hobnobbed with every kind of evil spirit, yet they do not even notice that they are spattered and befouled with mud.

But now let us leave this question and get back to the lesson we can draw every day from nutrition. Every creature is like a fruit or some other kind of food, and we must retain only what is tasty and digestible in it. God has placed a spark in each being, and we must try to establish a relationship with that spark, and not with all the rest. If you cease to look only at the outer aspects, you may even discover a spark in animals, plants and rocks. Every single creature possesses that inner spark. Sometimes it is buried very deep, but it is there, even in a criminal; and if you know how to arouse it and stir it to life, you can communicate and establish a relationship with it.

An initiate has no wish to relate to the lower nature of human beings, to their personality. He knows that if he goes down to their basements he will find only rats and mildew, and that he will be better off on the upper floors. In sharp contrast to ordinary human beings who are only interested in other peoples defects – who even get together to discuss them – an initiate hunts for the divine spark buried in each person and works to reunite it with the heavenly Father and the divine Mother. This is how a Master works to influence people, and one day light dawns in them. This is how he works on his disciples, nurturing the divine spark within them until it awakens, and this is why disciples love their Master, because he speaks only to what is best in them.

You can do the same: when you meet other human beings, try to seek out that hidden spark, their higher self, and help them to renew and strengthen their bond with the Lord. This is the most highly evolved, the loftiest form of love: to relate only to the divine spark in each human being so as to nurture and reinforce it. If you do this you need never be on your guard against others or waste time studying them before loving them, for that spark is all-pure. Where the personality is concerned it is better to know people before accepting them as your friends, but you can immediately accept the divine spark that shines in each human being.

II

Men and women can be compared to fruit –
this I have already told you – and when you are
in touch with them, when you look at them, talk
or listen to them it is as though you were tasting
them. But what is it that you are tasting most of
the time? Their clothes? Their jewellery? Their
faces? Do you ever seek any deeper to discover
the hidden life of the soul and spirit within them?
And yet it is this that should interest you, not all
the rest. No, you are interested in what you can
see on the surface, and you say, 'Ah, what a lovely
girl; if only I could sleep with her,' and then you
take a photo. But what have you actually seen?
Because of your urge to satisfy your appetites and
have pleasure, you have seen only what appears
on the surface: her legs, her breasts, her delightful
little nose.

An initiate also needs to eat, but the food he
is looking for is divine life, so that when he finds
fruit or flowers – that is, men and women – in

whom he glimpses this life, instead of assaulting and devouring them, he is content to admire their colour and form and to breathe in the fragrance of their emanations. And he goes on his way happy, for they have enabled him to approach heaven.

If you understood the question of nutrition you would be able to solve all your problems, including the problem of sex. Yes, those who decide never to allow themselves any nourishment in this area – all those, that is, who flee the company of the opposite sex under the pretext of purity and chastity – die spiritually, and sometimes even physically. You must 'eat.' The only question is what to eat and how to eat.

The secret is to learn to eat only 'homeopathic' quantities, by which I mean to nourish oneself by looking, listening and breathing. One must never refuse to nourish oneself under the pretext of becoming a saint and drawing closer to the Lord, for then one will know neither the Lord nor anything else. In fact, life will seep away and there one will be, stranded, with no enthusiasm, no inspiration, no joy. Holiness, sanctity, is food, my dear brothers and sisters; this is what initiates have understood. Instead of eating heavy, stodgy, impure food, they eat only what is divine. Where sexuality is concerned, human beings always go to extremes: either they starve themselves to death or they pounce on this 'food' and stuff themselves until they are sick.

You will find the solution to all this once you begin to study nutrition and the different ways in which we nourish ourselves on the different levels. You will learn that we cannot live without eating, and that even the angels, even the Lord has to eat. The Lord is nourished by the subtlest emanations of the trees he has planted, that is, by the emanations of all his creatures. Yes, I assure you, the Lord does eat: he eats his own kind of food and thrives on it. He thrives on it because he knows the correct way to eat and never consumes anything impure. He leaves the impurities for others to transform before they are brought to him.

You are wondering how you can tell whether someone eats correctly or not. Well, how can you tell whether someone is a beggar who finds his food in rubbish bins or a prince whose table is always loaded with the choicest dishes? It is the same on the spiritual level. Initiates look different from other people because they have a proper diet, whereas others eat anything that comes to hand.

Personally, I have a criterion by which to judge: when I see someone with no light in his face I know that he is 'undernourished.' You may say, 'But he goes to church, he gives alms to the poor, he never raises his eyes to a woman.' All that may be true, but I can see that, internally, he eats rotten meat. Whereas if I see someone who radiates light, whatever anyone else may tell me about him,

I say to myself, 'Now, there's someone who has a secret, and I mean to learn his secret because it is obviously an abundant source.' You may say, 'But I saw him on the beach, looking at the girls.' That makes no difference. What counts is what he is looking for and what he finds.

If a man's awe and admiration of the beauty of women helps him to rise heavenward, why should you want to stop him? 'But someone who is pure, a saint, would never do that. He should stick to the age-old rules.' Ah, I see. But then you, who are all purity and holiness, why are you so weak and lifeless? Why do you have no enthusiasm, no inspiration? How is it that your sanctity has not given you these things? And how is it that what you call his licentiousness has brought him light and heaven itself? No, no! There is something here that must be looked into a little more closely. This is just one example that shows that people do not know how to think or reason correctly.

Life is based on symbiosis: relationships of exchange. Exchanges with food, water, air, human beings; exchanges with all the creatures of the universe, with the angels and with God himself. When I speak of exchanges I am not only speaking of nourishment, of eating and drinking. Or rather, yes: I am speaking of eating and drinking but in all dimensions, not only on the physical plane. So, when I say that nutrition has to take first place, I am speaking of nutrition on every level, I am speaking of the interaction and exchanges we must have with all the different regions of the universe in order to nourish every aspect of our being, from the physical to the subtlest of our bodies. If I often insist on the necessity of purification, both on the physical and on the psychic level, it is because purity restores communications, and once communications have been restored we can tune in to the currents of luminous energy circulating through the universe.

Prayer, meditation, contemplation and ecstasy are all forms of nutrition. They are the best and most sublime forms, in fact, for they give us a taste of celestial food, of ambrosia. All religions speak of a drink that bestows immortality, that which alchemists called the Elixir of everlasting life, and it is true that this Elixir can be found on the physical level, but only on condition that we look for it in the highest, purest regions.

This is exactly what we are doing when we go to contemplate the sun as it rises: we are there to drink the ambrosia that pours from the sun into every nook and cranny of the world. Together with the rocks, plants, animals and all other creatures, we are there to receive some particles of sunlight. In fact, plants are more intelligent than human beings, for they renew contact with the sun every single day so as to be sure to bear fruit, whereas human beings sleep until noon, and if they watch the sun at all it is at sunset. Instead of looking at something that is mounting, blossoming, expanding, they prefer to watch something that is sinking, dying and fading. And as there is a law which decrees that we end by resembling whatever we love and contemplate, they, too, begin to fade and weaken and die inwardly.

The very meaning of life is concealed in nutrition, and if you take care to allow only the purest particles, only the most luminous, celestial, eternal quintessences into your inner fortress, this meaning will become clear to you. You will find these particles in the sun. This is why I tell you to concentrate on the sun every morning; try to breathe in and absorb the quintessences the sun sheds all around it. And you will see that your health will improve, you will have a clearer intelligence, your heart will experience greater joy and your will-power will be strengthened.

You will say that you have been going to see the sun rise for years now, and that you have never felt anything special. That is because you do not know how to look at it; it is the way you do things, the intensity of love and concentration you bring to your actions that gets results, not the time you spend on them. If you feel so vitalized, so fulfilled today, it is simply because you have drunk from that inexhaustible source, the sun. Is that so difficult to understand?

The sun is food, my dear brothers and sisters, never forget that, the very best food that exists. Why restrict your nourishment to the elements of earth, water and air? You must learn to nourish yourselves with fire and light; this is what we practise every morning at sunrise. When Zarathustra asked Ahura Mazda what food the first man ate, Ahura Mazda replied: 'He ate fire and drank light.' This fire and light are the rays of the sun and the life that pours from it, and it is thanks to them that we shall understand all the mysteries of the universe.

III

And now, if I tell you that the laws that govern nutrition are identical with those that govern conception, you will once again be astonished, because you have certainly never seen the correspondence between the two. But that correspondence exists: when you eat you create the conditions required for the birth of thoughts, feelings and actions. If you do not eat, what can you hope to accomplish? And just as the state of mind of the father and mother during conception determines the destiny of their future baby, similarly, your state of mind while you eat determines the nature of your physical and psychic activity. With every mouthful that you eat, a 'child' is conceived, and what is your state of mind at that moment of conception? Food is the live germ that will produce a child – that is, thoughts, feelings and actions. What kind of forces will be born of this union? Will your children be deformed, unhealthy and weak because of the ignorance of their father and mother? Each one of you is the father, because it is you who supplies the food, and your physical body is the mother. If the father and mother are not attentive, intelligent and sensible the results will be disastrous.

If you eat while feeling troubled, angry or discontented, you will experience a kind of feverishness, a disorder in your vibrations when you go back to work, and this disorder will be communicated to everything you do. Even if you try to give the impression that you are perfectly calm and in control, others will sense a certain confusion and tension emanating from you. But if you are in a state of harmony while eating, that state will remain with you afterwards. Even if you have to race from one activity to another, you will feel your peace still there within you; it will not be destroyed by your activity.

Never take your worries and cares to meals with you, therefore; leave them at the door and later, if you feel you really must, you can pick them up again. After eating in the right conditions you will more easily find solutions to your problems. I repeat: meals are an occasion for the best possible spiritual exercises. Begin them, therefore, by banishing from your mind whatever might prevent you from eating in peace and harmony. And if you do not succeed immediately, wait until you have managed to restore your inner calm, otherwise you will simply poison your food and end in a state of chaos, all because you have not eaten correctly.

But how can one get human beings to understand the importance of the right frame of mind while they eat, when one knows that some couples, even in the act of conceiving a child – which is, after all, an act of greater consequence – really detest each other? They do not realize what abominable things they are implanting in their child, and later on, that child will suffer and cause suffering to those around him.

Nutrition is a form of conception, and love is a form of nutrition. You must realize that heaven will hold you responsible for what you implant in the heart and soul of your partner. The rest does not matter so much. It is criminal to make love to your sweetheart when you are feeling depressed and miserable, thinking that this will make you feel better, because you will simply be relieving yourself by burdening her with your filth. So many people do this, but you must not choose that moment to make love. Love whomever you like, embrace whomever you like, but not before you have developed the very best of your heart and soul, your most luminous qualities, so that you can bestow them on the one you love. If you love in this way, heaven will never blame you. Human beings may blame you, perhaps, but heaven will applaud your behaviour.

After nine months in its mother's womb a child is born. Its umbilical cord is cut, and it can then feed itself independently. And yet, even when human beings leave their mother's womb they are still in the womb of another mother, mother nature, and they continue to be fed through that other umbilical cord, the solar plexus. In India, China and Japan, there are some very ancient techniques for learning to nourish oneself by means of the solar plexus. I know that you would love to hear about them, but what would you do with them if you are still not capable of eating according to the rules I have explained to you?

It is impossible not to be struck with awe and admiration when one sees how marvellously divine intelligence has arranged everything. Just think: you eat some fruit and through the process of digestion and assimilation that fruit contributes to the life of your whole organism. What intelligence is this, that is capable of giving every single organ exactly what it needs in order to keep our bodies alive and well? Thanks to this food, we continue to see and hear, to breathe, to taste, touch and speak, to sing and to walk. And even hair and nails, teeth and skin receive the nourishment they need to go on growing.

Truly, an intelligence such as this commands our admiration. From now on, try to think about this intelligence more often. Try to get to know it, to establish a bond with it, to express your gratitude to it, and even, from time to time, ask to be allowed to watch the work that it is accomplishing throughout nature. Yes, for as soon as you are fully prepared, you may be invited to visit some of the innumerable workshops of this sublime intelligence and see it at work, whether in your own body or in the bowels of the earth, where minerals, metals, crystals and precious stones are being fashioned. When that time comes you will make some real discoveries.

Where do you suppose that initiatic science comes from? It was given to us by beings who had developed powers of bilocation that enabled them to explore the interior of the earth and the oceans, the other planets, and even the sun itself, where they found an extraordinary variety of life such as human beings could never imagine. Yes, for the sun is a land inhabited by the most luminous, the most highly evolved creatures. It is the *Aretz ha Haim* of the Psalms, the 'Land of the Living.'

These very advanced spirits, having travelled through all the reaches of space and visited every area of the universe, bequeathed to us this science that I am now handing on to you. To reassure you, let me tell you that I know very little of it as yet, but one day I hope to know more.

Izvor Collection

201 - Toward a Solar Civilization
It is not enough to be familiar with the astronomical theory of heliocentricity. Since the sun is the centre of our universe, we must learn to put it at the centre of all our preoccupations and activities.

202 - Man, Master of His Destiny
If human beings are to be masters of their own destiny, they must understand that the laws which govern their physical, psychic and spiritual life are akin to those which govern the universe.

203 - Education Begins Before Birth
Humanity will improve and be transformed only when people realize the true import of the act of conception. In this respect, men and women have a tremendous responsibility for which they need years of preparation.

204 - The Yoga of Nutrition
The way we eat is as important as what we eat. Through our thoughts and feelings, it is possible to extract from our food spiritual elements which can contribute to the full flowering of our being.

205 - Sexual Force or the Winged Dragon
How to master, domesticate and give direction to our sexual energy so as to soar to the highest spheres of the spirit.

206 - A Philosophy of Universality
We must learn to replace our restricted, self-centred point of view with one that is immensely broad and universal. If we do this we shall all benefit; not only materially but particularly on the level of consciousness.

207 - What is a Spiritual Master
A true spiritual Master is, first, one who is conscious of the essential truths written by cosmic intelligence into the great book of Nature. Secondly, he must have achieved complete mastery of the elements of his own being. Finally, all the knowledge and authority he has acquired must serve only to manifest the qualities and virtues of selfless love.

208 - The Egregor of the Dove or the Reign of Peace
Peace will finally reign in the world only when human beings work to establish peace within themselves, in their every thought, feeling and action.

209 - Christmas and Easter in the Initiatic Tradition
Human beings are an integral part of the cosmos and intimately concerned by the process of gestation and birth going on in nature. Christmas and Easter – rebirth and resurrection – are simply two ways of envisaging humanity's regeneration and entry into the spiritual life.

210 - The Tree of the Knowledge of Good and Evil

Methods, not explanations, are the only valid answers to the problem of evil. Evil is an inner and outer reality which confronts us every day, and we must learn to deal with it.

211 - Freedom, the Spirit Triumphant

A human being is a spirit, a spark sprung from within the Almighty. Once a person understands, sees and feels this truth, he will be free.

212 - Light is a Living Spirit

Light, the living matter of the universe, is protection, nourishment and an agency for knowledge for human beings. Above all, it is the only truly effective means of self-transformation.

213 - Man's Two Natures, Human and Divine

Man is that ambiguous creature that evolution has placed on the borderline between the animal world and the divine world. His nature is ambivalent, and it is this ambivalence that he must understand and overcome.

214 - Hope for the World: Spiritual Galvanoplasty

On every level of the universe, the masculine and feminine principles reproduce the activity of those two great cosmic principles known as the Heavenly Father and the Divine Mother of which every manifestation of nature and life are a reflection. Spiritual galvanoplasty is a way of applying the science of these two fundamental principles to one's inner life.

215 - The True Meaning of Christ's Teaching

Jesus incorporated into the Our Father - or Lord's Prayer - an ancient body of knowledge handed down by Tradition and which had existed long before his time. A vast universe is revealed to one who knows how to interpret each of the requests formulated in this prayer.

216 - The Living Book of Nature

Everything in nature is alive and it is up to us to learn how to establish a conscious relationship with creation so as to receive that life within ourselves.

217 - New Light on the Gospels

The Parables and other tales from the Gospels are here interpreted as situations and events applicable to our own inner life.

218 - The Symbolic Language of Geometrical Figures

Each geometrical figure – circle, triangle, pentagram, pyramid or cross – is seen as a structure fundamental to the organization of the macrocosm (the universe) and the microcosm (human beings).

219 - Man's Subtle Bodies and Centres

However highly developed our sense organs, their scope will never reach beyond the physical plane. To experience richer and subtler sensations, human beings must exercise the subtler organs and spiritual centres that they also possess: the aura, the solar plexus, the Hara centre, the Chakras, and so on.

220 - The Zodiac, Key to Man and to the Universe

Those who are conscious of being part of the universe feel the need to work inwardly in order to find within themselves the fullness of the cosmic order so perfectly symbolized by the Zodiac.

221 - True Alchemy or The Quest for Perfection

Instead of fighting our weaknesses and vices – we would inevitably be defeated – we must learn to make them work for us. We think it normal to harness the untamed forces of nature, so why be surprised when a Master, an initiate, speaks of harnessing the primitive forces within us? This is true spiritual alchemy.

222 - Man's Psychic Life: Elements and Structures

"Know thyself." How to interpret this precept carved over the entrance to the temple at Delphi? To know oneself is to be conscious of one's different bodies, from the denser to the most subtle, of the principles which animate these bodies, of the needs they induce in one, and of the state of consciousness which corresponds to each.

223 - Creation: Artistic and Spiritual

Everyone needs to create but true creation involves spiritual elements. Artists, like those who seek the spirit, have to reach beyond themselves in order to receive elements from the higher planes.

224 - The Powers of Thought

Thought is a power, an instrument given to us by God so that we may become creators like himself – creators in beauty and perfection. This means that we must be extremely watchful, constantly verifying that what we do with our thoughts is truly for our own good and that of the whole world. This is the one thing that matters.

225 - Harmony and Health

Illness is a result of some physical or psychic disorder. The best defence against illness, therefore, is harmony. Day and night we must take care to be attuned and in harmony with life as a whole, with the boundless life of the cosmos.

226 - The Book of Divine Magic

True, divine magic, consists in never using the faculties, knowledge, or powers one has acquired for one's own self-interest, but always and only for the establishment of God's kingdom on earth.

227 - Golden Rules for Everyday Life

Why spoil one's life by chasing after things that matter less than life itself? Those who learn to give priority to life, who protect and preserve it in all integrity, will find more and more that they obtain their desires. For it is this, an enlightened, luminous life that can give them everything.

228 - Looking into the Invisible

Meditation, dreams, visions, astral projection all give us access to the invisible world, but the quality of the revelations received depends on our efforts to elevate and refine our perceptions.

229 - The Path of Silence

In every spiritual teaching, practices such as meditation and prayer have only one purpose: to lessen the importance attributed to one's lower nature and give one's divine nature more and more scope for expression. Only in this way can a human being experience true silence.

230 - The Book of Revelations: A Commentary

If *Revelations* is a difficult book to interpret it is because we try to identify the people, places and events it describes instead of concentrating on the essence of its message: a description of the elements and processes of our spiritual life in relation to the life of the cosmos.

231 - The Seeds of Happiness

Happiness is like a talent which has to be cultivated. Those who want to possess happiness must go in search of the elements which will enable them to nourish it inwardly; elements which belong to the divine world.

232 - The Mysteries of Fire and Water

Our psychic life is fashioned every day by the forces we allow to enter us, the influences that impregnate us. What could be more poetic, more meaningful than water and fire and the different forms under which they appear?

233 - Youth: Creators of the Future

Youth is full of life, enthusiasms and aspirations of every kind. The great question is how to channel its extraordinary, overflowing effervescence of energies.

234 - Truth, Fruit of Wisdom and Love –

We all abide by our own "truth", and it is in the name of their personal "truth" that human beings are continually in conflict. Only those who possess true love and true wisdom discover the same truth and speak the same language.

235 - In Spirit and in Truth

Since we live on earth we are obliged to give material form to our religious beliefs. Sacred places and objects, rites, prayers and ceremonies are expressions of those beliefs. It is important to understand that they are no more than expressions – expressions which are always more or less inadequate. They are not themselves the religion, for religion exists in spirit and in truth.

236 - Angels and Other Mysteries of the Tree of Life

God is like a pure current of electricity which can reach us only through a series of transformers. These transformers are the countless luminous beings which inhabit the heavens and which tradition calls the Angelic Hierarchies. It is through them that we receive divine life; through them that we are in contact with God.

237 - Cosmic Balance, the Secret of Polarity

Libra - the Scales - symbolizes cosmic balance, the equilibrium of the two opposite and complementary forces, the masculine and feminine principles, by means of which the universe came into being and continues to exist. The symbolism of Libra, expression of this twofold polarity, dominates the whole of creation.

238 - The Faith That Moves Mountains

Faith is the result of an age-old knowledge buried deep within our subconscious. It is founded on an experience of the divine world, an experience which has left indelible traces on each one of us and which we must reanimate.

239 - Love Greater Than Faith

As long as we have not understood what true faith is, there can be no love; and conversely, as long as we do not know how to manifest love, we cannot claim that we have faith.

240 - Sons and Daughters of God

'Two thousand years ago, the coming of Jesus introduced a new order of things where, for the first time in human history, the values of love, goodness, forgiveness, patience, gentleness, humility and sacrifice were put in first place. And even if Jesus' words have not yet been either completely understood or practised, it has been enough that certain beings have received this light for it to be transmitted down through the centuries. The love for one's neighbour which was taught by Jesus and which stems from this truth that humans are sons and daughters of the same Father has allowed the idea of brotherhood to forge a path.'

Books by Omraam Mikhaël Aïvanhov
(translated from the French)

Complete Works

Volume 1 – The Second Birth
Volume 2 – Spiritual Alchemy
Volume 5 – Life Force
Volume 6 – Harmony
Volume 7 – The Mysteries of Yesod
Volume 10 – The Splendour of Tiphareth
The Yoga of the Sun
Volume 11 – The Key to the Problems of Existence
Volume 12 – Cosmic Moral Laws
Volume 13 – A New Earth
Methods, Exercises, Formulas, Prayers
Volume 14 – Love and Sexuality (Part I)
Volume 15 – Love and Sexuality (Part II)
Volume 17 – 'Know Thyself' Jnana Yoga (Part I)
Volume 18 – 'Know Thyself' Jnana Yoga (Part II)
Volume 25 – A New Dawn:
Society and Politics in the Light of Initiatic Science (Part I)
Volume 26 – A New Dawn:
Society and Politics in the Light of Initiatic Science (Part II)
Volume 29 – On the Art of Teaching (Part III)
Volume 30 – Life and Work in an Initiatic School
Training for the Divine
Volume 32 – The Fruits of the Tree of Life
The Cabbalistic Tradition

Brochures

301 – The New Year
302 – Meditation
303 – Respiration
304 – Death and the Life Beyond

World Wide - Editor-Distributor
Editions Prosveta S.A. - Z.A. Le Capitou - B.P. 12
F - 83601 Fréjus CEDEX (France)
Tel. (33) 04 94 19 33 33 – Fax (33) 04 94 19 33 34
Web: www.prosveta.com – e-mail: international@prosveta.com

Distributors

AUSTRALIA
PROSVETA Australia
P.O. Box 538 – Mittagong – N.S.W. 2575 Australia

AUSTRIA
HARMONIEQUELL VERSAND – Hof 37 – A- 5302 Henndorf am Wallersee
Tel. / fax (43) 6214 7413 – e-mail: info@prosveta.at

BELGIUM & LUXEMBOURG
PROSVETA BENELUX – Beeldenmakersstraat 1 – B 8000 Brugge
Tel./Fax. (32)(0)50/61 69 10 – e-mail : prosveta@skynet.be
N.V. MAKLU Somersstraat 13-15 – B-2000 Antwerpen
Tel. (32) 3/231 29 00 – Fax (32) 3/233 26 59
VANDER S.A. – Av. des Volontaires 321 – B-1150 Bruxelles
Tel. (32)(0)2 732 35 32 – Fax. (32) (0)2 732 42 74 – e-mail: g.i.a@wol.be

BULGARIA
SVETOGLED – Bd Saborny 16 A, appt 11 – 9000 Varna
e-mail: vassil100@abv.bg – Tel/Fax: (359) 52 63 90 94

CANADA
PROSVETA Inc. – 3950, Albert Mines – Canton-de-Hatley (Qc), J0B 2C0
Tel. (819) 564-8212 – Fax. (819) 564-1823 – *in Canada,* call toll free: 1-800-854-8212
e-mail: prosveta@prosveta-canada.com / www.prosveta-canada.com

CONGO
PROSVETA CONGO
29, Avenue de la Révolution – B.P. 768 – Pointe-Noire
Tel. : (242) 948156 / (242) 5531254 – Fax : (242) 948156
e-mail: prosvetacongo@yahoo.fr

COLOMBIA
PROSVETA – Calle 149 N° 24 B - 20 – Bogotá
Tel. (57) 1 614 88 28 – Tel. (57) 1 614 53 85 – Fax (57) 1 633 58 03
Mobile (57) 311 810 25 42 – e-mail: kalagiya@tutopia.com

CYPRUS
THE SOLAR CIVILISATION BOOKSHOP – BOOKBINDING
73 D Kallipoleos Avenue – Lycavitos – P. O. Box 24947, 1355 – Nicosia
e-mail: cypapach@cytanet.com.cy – Tel / Fax 00357-22-377503

CZECH REPUBLIC
PROSVETA – Ant. Sovy 18 – České Budejovice 370 05
Tel / Fax: (420) 38-53 10 227 – e-mail: prosveta@iol.cz

FRANCE – DOM TOM
Editions Prosveta S.A. - B.P. 12 – F - 83601 Fréjus CEDEX (France)
Tel. (33) 04 94 19 33 33 – Fax (33) 04 94 19 33 34
e-mail: international@prosveta.com – www.prosveta.com

GERMANY
PROSVETA Verlag GmbH – Heerstrasse 55 – 78628 Rottweil
Tel. (49) 741-46551 – Fax. (49) 741-46552 – e-mail: prosveta7@aol.com

GREAT BRITAIN – IRELAND
PROSVETA – The Doves Nest, Duddleswell Uckfield – East Sussex TN 22 3JJ
Tel. (44) (01825) 712988 – Fax (44) (01825) 713386 – e-mail: prosveta@pavilion.co.uk

GREECE
RAOMRON – D. RAGOUSSIS
3, rue A. Papamdreou – C.P. 16675 – Glifada - Athenes
Tel / Fax: (010) 9681127 – e-mail: raomron@hol.gr

HAITI

PROSVETA DÉPÔT HAITI – Angle rue Faustin 1ᵉʳ et rue Bois Patate #25 bis
6110 Port-au-Prince – Haiti
Tol. (509) 245 18 65 – Tel. (509) 404 88 88 – e-mail: rbaaudant@yahoo.com

HOLLAND

STICHTING PROSVETA NEDERLAND
Zeestraat 50 – 2042 LC Zandvoort
Tel. (31) 33 25 345 75 – Fax. (31) 33 25 803 20 – e-mail: prosveta@worldonline.nl

ISRAEL

Zohar, P.B. 1046, Netanya 42110 – e-mail: zohar7@012.net.il

ITALY

PROSVETA Coop. a r.l.
Casella Postale 55 – 06068 Tavernelle (PG)
Tel. (39) 075-835 84 98 – Fax (39) 075-835 97 12 – e-mail: prosveta@tin.it

IVORY COAST

Librairie Prosveta
25 rue Paul Langevin Zone 4C – 01 Abidjan
e-mail: prosvetafrique@yahoo.fr – Tel/Fax: (225) 21 25 42 11

LEBANON

PROSVETA LIBAN – P.O. Box 90-995
Jdeidet-el-Metn, Beirut – Tel. (03) 448560 – e-mail: prosveta_lb@terra.net.lb

NORWAY

PROSVETA NORDEN – Postboks 318, N-1502 Moss
Tel. (47) 69 26 51 40 – Fax (47) 69 26 51 08 – e-mail: prosnor@online.no

PORTUGAL

EDIÇÕES PROSVETA
Rua Passos Manuel, n° 20 – 3ᵉ E, P 1150 – 260 Lisboa
Tel. (351) (21) 354 07 64 – Fax (351) (21) 798 60 31
e-mail : prosvetapt@hotmail.com

ROMANIA

ANTAR – Str. N. Constantinescu 10 – Bloc 16A - sc A - Apt. 9
Sector 1 – 71253 Bucarest
Tel. 004021-231 28 78 – Tel./ Fax 004021-231 37 19
e-mail : prosveta_ro@yahoo.com

RUSSIA

EDITIONS PROSVETA
143 964 Moskovskaya oblast, g. Reutov – 4, post/box 4
Tel./ Fax. (095) 525 18 17 – Tel. (095) 795 70 74 – e-mail: prosveta@online.ru

SPAIN

ASOCIACIÓN PROSVETA ESPAÑOLA – C/ Ausias March n° 23 Ático
SP-08010 Barcelona – Tel (34) (93) 412 31 85 – Fax (34) (93) 318 89 01
e-mail: aprosveta@prosveta.es

UNITED STATES

PROSVETA US Dist. – PO Box 2125 – Canyon Country CA 91386
Tél. (661)252-1751 – Fax. (661) 252-9090
e-mail: prosveta-usa@earthlink.net / www.prosveta-usa.com

SWITZERLAND

PROSVETA Société Coopérative
Ch. de la Céramone 3A – CH - 1808 Les Monts-de-Corsier
Tel. (41) 21 921 92 18 – Fax. (41) 21 922 92 04
e-mail: prosveta@swissonline.ch

VENEZUELA

PROSVETA VENEZUELA C. A. – Calle Madrid
Edificio La Trinidad – Las Mercedes – Caracas D.F.
Tel. (58) 414 22 36 748 – e-mail: prosveta_venezuela@hotmail.com

If you cannot contact one of these distributors,
consult the internet site www.prosveta.com

The aim of the Universal White Brotherhood association
is the study and practice of the Teaching
of Master Omraam Mikhaël Aïvanhov,
published and distributed
by Prosveta.

All enquiries about the association should be addressed to:
Universal White Brotherhood
The Doves Nest, Duddleswell, Uckfield
East Sussex TN22 3JJ, GREAT BRITAIN
Tel: (44) (0)1825 712150 – Fax: (44) (0)1825 713386
E-mail: uwb@pavilion.co.uk

―――――――――――

Printed in march 2006
by DUMAS-TITOULET Imprimeurs
42004 Saint-Etienne – France

―――――――

Dépôt légal: mars 2006 – N° 43698C
1er dépôt légal dans la même collection en France: 1982